The Ghana Kente

Evolution

The Ghana Kente

Evolution

The evolution of the Ghana Bonwire Kente cloth. The meanings of the cloth names, the design names, and the colors used in Kente cloth weaving.

Richard Antwi-Boasiako

The Ghana Kente Evolution

raboasiako@optonline.net

Friday, September 11, 2020

E-ISBN: (978-0-578-77975-1)

ISBN: (978-0-578-77974-4)

Library of Congress Control Number: 2020919906

Printed in the United States of America

Dedication

My loving wife

Dr. Hermina Antwi-Boasiako

Our loving children

Richard Antwi-Boasiako

Leslie Antwi-Boasiako

Rachel Antwi-Boasiako

Acknowledgement

I thank my sisters-in-law Gladys Ofori, a teacher in Schenectady, New York and Paulina Mensah, a Nurse Practitioner in Houston, Texas for proofreading this book and correcting all my archaic grammar.

I thank my daughter Rachel Antwi-Boasiako and my wife Dr. Hermina Antwi-Boasiako for checking all my sentences to make them more contemporary.

I also thank my late uncles Wofa Boateng and Wofa Sefa, both master weavers who introduced me to Kente weaving at a tender age of seven.

Finally, I thank my parents Samuel Kwame Antwi-Boasiako/Susana Owusua and my siblings for all the history lessons on our roots, especially the ones on our journey from Bonwire to Konongo to Asuom to Okyinso.

Table of Contents

"The old order changeth, yielding place to new, And God fulfills himself in many ways, Lest one good custom should corrupt the world. Comfort thyself: what comfort is in me? I have lived my life, and that which I have done May he within himself make pure! but thou, If thou shouldst never see my face again, Pray for my soul. More things are wrought by prayer than this world dreams of."

A quote from "The Passing of Arthur".

By Alfred Tennyson

Preface

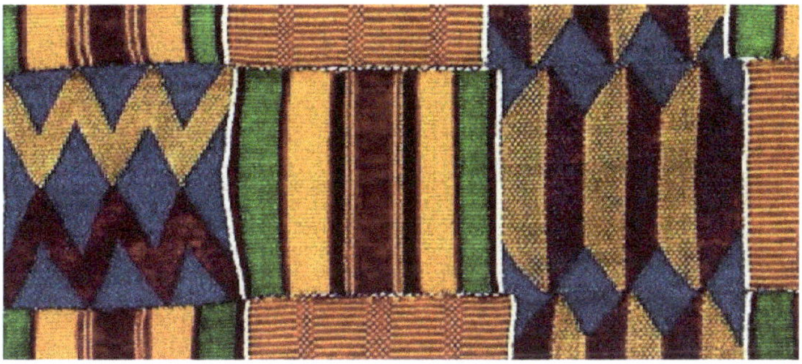

Kente cloth has been woven in Ghana for over 400 years. The tradition was handed down from one generation to the other through oral tradition and apprenticeship. Finding good literature on Kente cloth is not easy. Sadly, the original Kente cloth weavers did not document the practice. Most of the writings and documentaries can be attributed to people who are merely fascinated by it. The literature is based on what these writers were told when visiting any of the areas where Kente was woven or sold.

Growing up in a small village called Okyinso in Ghana, my family were the only Kente weavers in that area. My grandfather had migrated from Bonwire, the origin of the Kente cloth and settled there to ply his trade. He was also a medicine man (*Sumankwaa*). He taught some of his children the art of weaving Kente and others the art of using herbs to cure all kinds of ailments. My father was sent to school and could not be introduced to any of those professions, likewise his descendants.

This book was written to document the knowledge passed down by oral tradition and help keep this rich Kente weaving history alive. There are lots of tourists to Bonwire who share their experiences mostly as a video clip, to document the beauty of the Kente cloth. This book gives an in-depth knowledge of the history, the beauty, the names, and the meaning of some of the colors and designs that go into the weaving of Kente cloth. There are different areas of interest regarding the Kente cloth. Some are interested in the origin and history of Kente while others are fascinated by the meaning of the design names and colors.

Less time was spent on the history which is mostly oral tradition. This book concentrated on the meanings of the colors and the designs that are used. The colors have been quite consistent: yellow, black, red, and green. A named cloth can be replicated in so many shades. The colors do not determine the name of the cloth. The warp design (the designs that are repeated many times within a cloth) determines the name of the Kente cloth. The designs have also been quite static, but weavers still attempt to create new ones by altering the existing ones and giving it a new name. The more they try to make it look different though, the more it resembles the older ones. The old basic geometric designs are here to stay. They will always be a part of any beautiful Kente cloth.

There are a lot of videos on the internet about interviews of weavers and sellers from Bonwire. There seems to be a gradual degradation of the facts as they try to tell the Kente history from memory. The weavers have all the knowledge, but it will be difficult for them to write about it. The purpose of this book is to preserve this history with proper documentation to avoid this degradation. The beauty of the Kente cloth is in the colors and designs. This book has included a lot of color pictures because a picture is worth a thousand words. To talk about Kente cloth without a colored picture, is doing injustice to the culture.

It is my hope that this book will contribute to keeping the Kente weaving tradition well documented. My goal is that readers will use this book as a guide in their search for their cherished Kente cloth. Like any African market, the Kente cloth market can be intimidating. Visitors are presented with so many choices from a plethora of vendors that it becomes a nightmare deciding on which Kente to buy. Just going to a Kente store to pick up any Kente cloth without any research is therefore not encouraged. Know the name and meaning of the cloth you really admire before heading to the market. The beauty is always the number one thing that will attract a Kente cloth buyer which is good however, knowing the name and the meaning of the name of the cloth in addition is far better.

Chapter 1

Kente Cloth History

The origin of the name *Kente* is contested by two main tribes in Ghana namely the Asantes from Ashanti region in Ghana and the Ewes from the Volta region in Ghana. The Asantes claim Kente is derived from the Akan word "*Kenteng*" (which means basket) because the weaving and the final product looks like a basket. Another name the Asantes used for Kente is *Kenteng Ntoma* (meaning basket cloth). The Ewes claim Kente is from the Ewe word "*Kete*" which had been corrupted into Kente. In the Ewe language "*ke*" means to open and "*te*" means to tighten. Both tribes have incredibly beautiful Kente cloth. There are differences between Asante and Ewe Kente cloth. The Asante Kente has both sides of the cloth having the main design and looking identical. It is therefore difficult to differentiate the two sides. The Ewe Kente however has only one side showing the main design. This book is not meant to resolve the question of the origin of Kente but rather give you an insight into the Asante Bonwire Kente.

Asante history is mainly oral tradition and legend has it that two hunters Opoku Kurago and Kwakye Ameyaw from Asante Bonwire went hunting and observed a spider spinning a web. They studied this art of weaving by the spider which they mimicked in the weaving of Kente. The place where the spider was seen is now a historic site near Bonwire called *Ayewakeseho*. Kente weaving started around 1679 in Asante Bonwire. The first Kente cloth was black and white with thread from the raffia tree (*Edowa*). It was a bit uncomfortable on the skin, so the weavers decided to experiment with other materials. They found out that a local tree called *Onyina* (false-kapok tree) had pods full of a silky cotton-like substance that surrounds the seed. This was used to create the threads for the Kente cloth. With the expansion of the Asante kingdom through wars, places where actual cotton grew became part of the Asante empire and cotton became the preferred raw material for the threads.

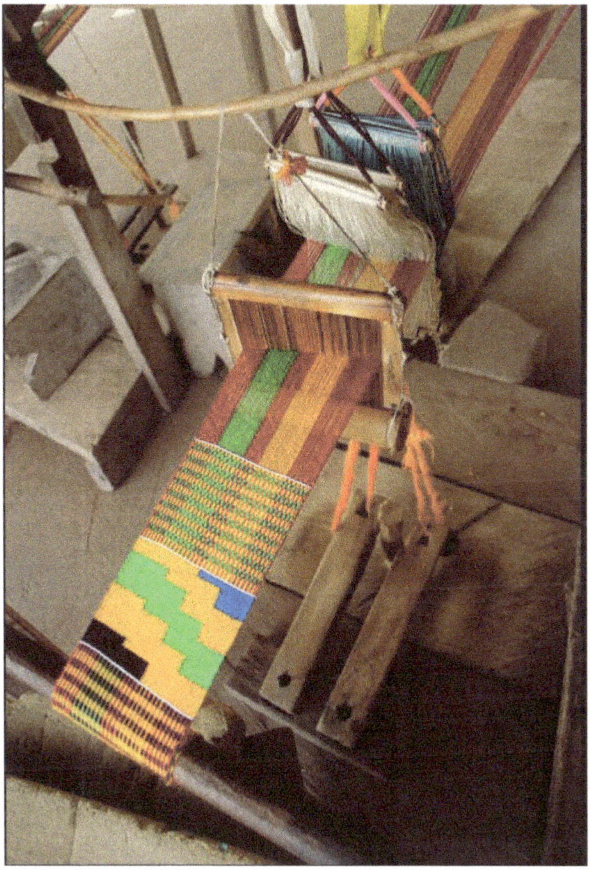

Kente Loom (Nsadua)

The evolution of Kente cloth can be grouped into three main phases. The first phase had quite a simple weaving system and the output was called *Ayaase Nwin-Ntoma* (waist woven cloth). With this system the weaver tied the threads around the two big toes of both legs and then tied it around the waist to form a triangular shape. Raffia fiber known locally as *edowa* was the main yarn. This was an important invention at that time, but raffia fibers were extremely uncomfortable on the skin.

The second phase also using the Raffia fibers produced what was called *Asaase-Nwin-Ntoma* (ground woven cloth). With this system, which was a big improvement of the first one, the weaver constructed three pegs on the ground in a triangular shape and tied the threads around them. This made the weaving easier and faster than the ones around the waist.

The third phase which is still in use produced what is called *Nsaduaso-Nwin-Ntoma* (loom woven cloth). This is the system of weaving the cloth in a loom. This system has seen extraordinarily little change. It is an amazingly simple but effective way of creating the Kente strips which are later joined to form the larger piece. The first cloth from the loom was called *Gagamuga.*

In the beginning, Kente cloth was woven only in black and white. When the European traders came to Ghana (then Gold Coast), Oyoko women traders were introduced to different fabric colors by these European traders and this revolutionized Kente weaving. These Oyoko women traders returned to Bonwire with colored head scarfs they bought from the Europeans. The black and white cloth evolved into the rich colorful cloth we have today. The introduction of color is credited to Nana Otaa Kraban the brother-in-law of Opoku Kurago and Kwakye Ameyaw. He was able to create different colors from the bark of trees. The bark of the tree was boiled with the white threads to turn them into rich colorful threads used in Kente weaving. The primary Kente colors were yellow, black, red, and green. The early Kente cloths after Nana Otaa Kraban's invention were colorful but had no designs until Nana Osei Kuffour came up with a way to weave geometric designs which is now part of every beautiful Kente.

Kente is mainly made from silk, rayon, and cotton. Silk is a slippery material and difficult to wear.

Most Kente weavers prefer rayon and cotton. Each geometric design and color have a specific meaning. The people from Bonwire taught other people in the areas they migrated how to weave Kente. The weaving of Kente therefore became widespread throughout Ghana especially the towns around Bonwire. However only few master weavers in Bonwire have the expertise to weave certain complex designs such as *Asasia and Nkontompo* Kente.

Another local name for the Kente Cloth is *nwin-ntoma* (meaning woven cloth). Every Kente starts as a long strip (*about 4 inches wide and 6 feet long*). These strips are later joined by hand or machine to create a larger piece. The men cloth normally uses 28 of these strips and the women need about 24 strips. Both the colors and the designs have special significance and meaning to the Asante people.

There are three main types of weaving Kente, namely Single, Double and Triple weave. A single weave Kente has no designs in it. It takes the least amount of time and is the cheapest. The local name is *Ahwrepan.* A double weave Kente has some designs in each block. This is the most popular as it is affordable to most people. The local name is *Topreko*. A triple weave Kente is the most time-consuming type. Each block is completely made up of designs. The local name is *Topreno*. Another name for a triple weave is *Edwin Si Edwin So* meaning design after design. It is as expected, the most expensive. A triple weave Kente cloth used to be called *Wabo bra* meaning you have made it in life.

There are the traditional Kente designs and the contemporary designs. The Kente weaver sits in a Kente loom and uses both hands and feet to control the weaving. The intended design for the cloth determines the colors of thread and symbols used. The repeated design normally determines the name of the cloth. Different cloths may have some designs that are the same but the patterns in which the designs are used eventually determines the name of the cloth. The weaver usually names the Kente cloth. Recently though, some Kente cloths have been renamed to commemorate an occasion or when a prominent person uses it. Names like Obama Kente and Fathia Fata Nkrumah are rebranding for existing Kente cloths.

All stools (Chieftaincy) in the Asante Kingdom are created by the Kings of Asante. There are several stools created in connection with Kente weaving. Stools in connection with Kente are placed under the *Gyaase* division of the Asante Kings court. There are currently *Kentehene* (Kente Chief), *Yokomaahene* (Chief of the color Kente), *Awinfohene* (Kente Design Chief), and *Fufutomahene* (White dominated Kente Chief).

Traditionally, custom demands that all the Asantehene's Kente be made only at Bonwire through the Kente Chiefs. The designed Asantehene Kente cloths were not permitted to be woven for any other person even if one could afford it. With time this tradition is gradually becoming obsolete and one can find some of the Asantehene's Kente cloth on sale to the public.

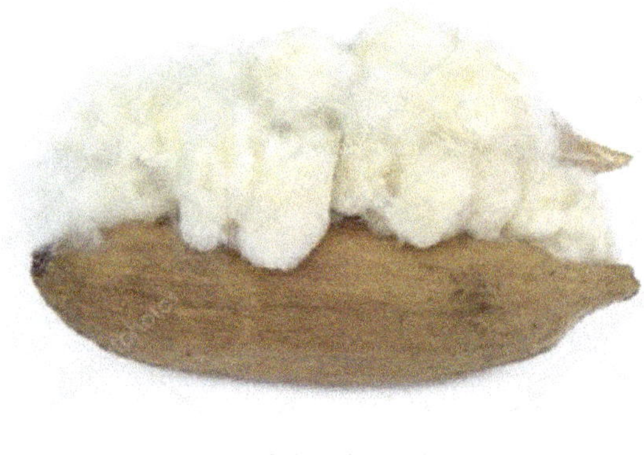

Onyina (false-kapok tree) pods

Chapter 2
Kente Cloth Loom

Kente cloth loom is a remarkably simple tool for making expensive cloth. The local name for the loom is *Nsadua*. The main features of the loom are listed below:

1. Shuttle and Bobbin – These hold the thread that is passed through the horizontal warp threads. The local names are *Krokrowa and Dodrowa.*

2. Beater – The main function of the Beater is to hold the threads very tight as one weaves. The local name is *Chereye*.

3. Heddles – Right behind the Beater are the Heddles. There are the main heddles and the pattern heddles. There may be two or more heddles depending on the complexity of the design. These are used with a Paddle to open the warp threads. For a typical cloth for the

Asantehene, one will use about six heddles or more. The local name is *Asa.*

4. Treadles – These are used by the toes to pull the Beater and heddles. The local name is *Ntiamo.*

5. Heddle Pulley – This is found at the top of the loom. It has a spool that makes it easier to pull the Heddles. The local name is *Donowa.*

6. Cloth Beam – This is placed on the top of the thighs close to the waist to wrap the finished cloth around. The local name is *Ayaase Dua.*

7. Measure Stick – This is used to measure the length to determine when to change the design. The local name is *Susu Dua.*

8. Drag Stone – This is a huge stone used to hold the warp threads at the opposite end of the loom. It maintains proper tension in the warp threads.

9. Paddle – This is used to open the warp threads.

When the great Ghanaian song writer Dr. Ephraim Koku Amu visited Bonwire, he composed his famous song called Bonwire Kente. According to his account, every house he visited in Bonwire had similar sound. The Kente weaving noise which sounded like *Kro-Kro-Kro-Kro He-He-He-He*. This is the sound as the weaver passes the shuttle and bobbin through the warp threads and then uses the toes to pull the heddles.

Loom Shuttle and Bobbin

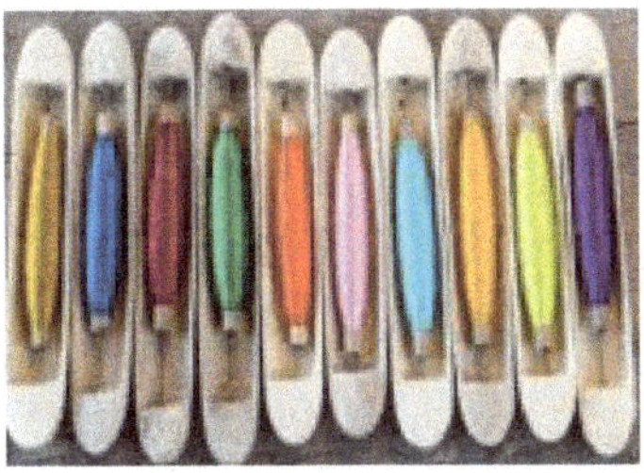

Loom Treadles

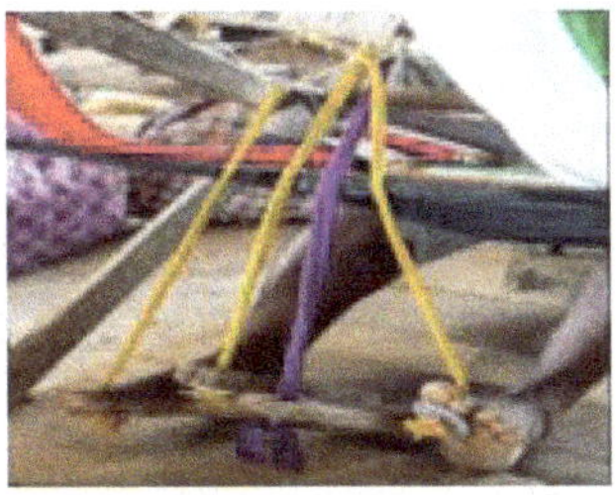

Loom Heddle Pulley

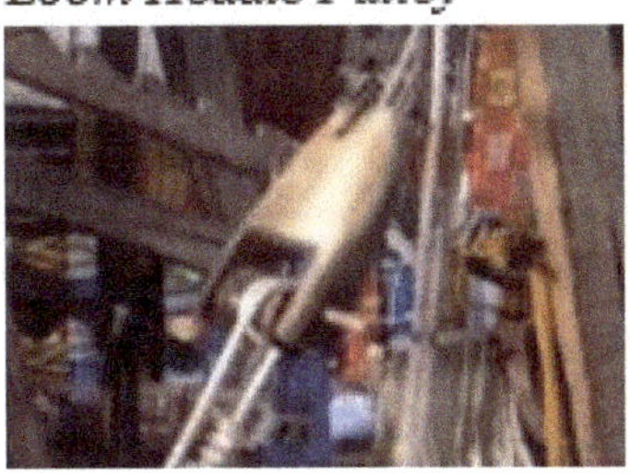

Loom Beater and Heddles

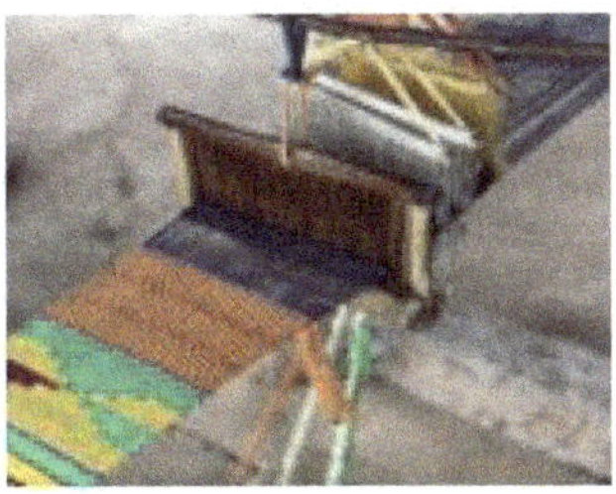

Loom Cloth Beam

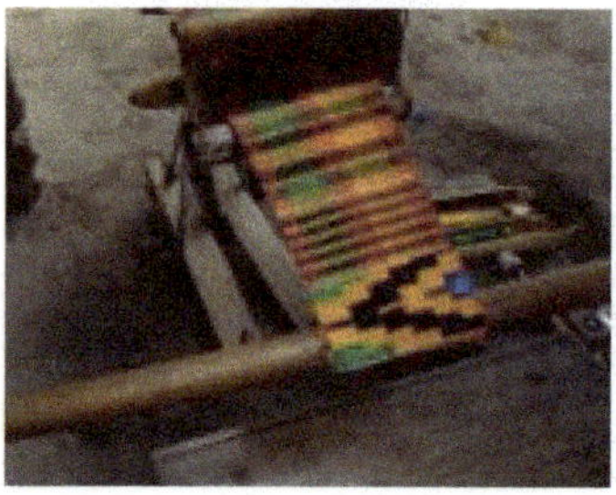

Loom Paddle

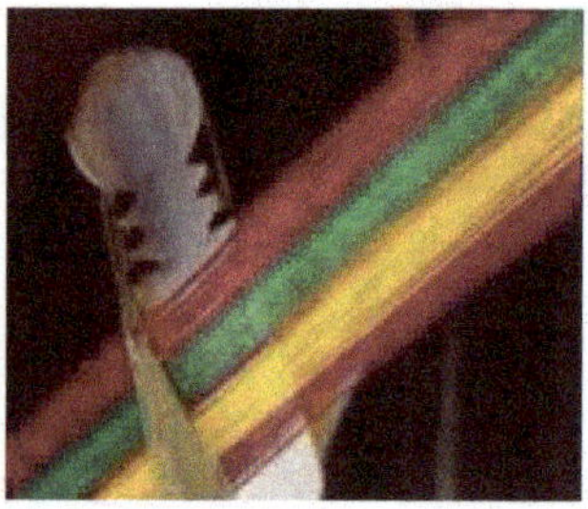

Kente Loom (Nsadua)

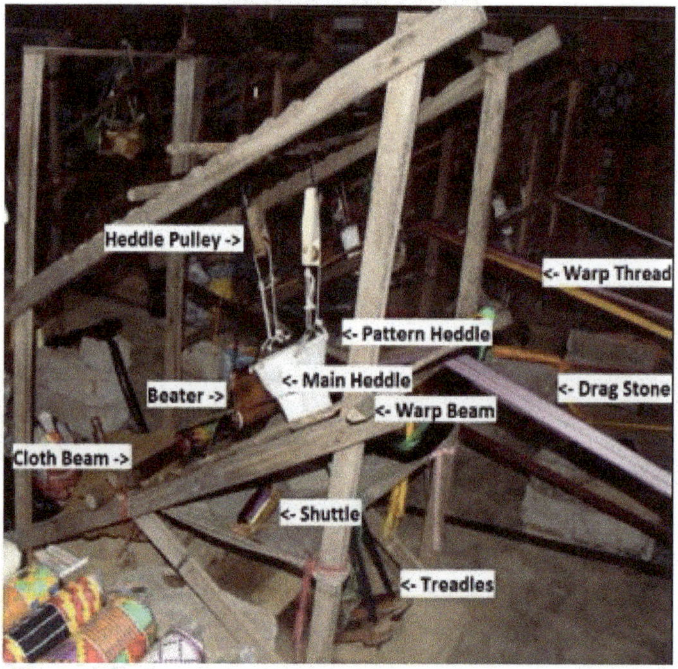

Chapter 3

Kente Cloth Colors

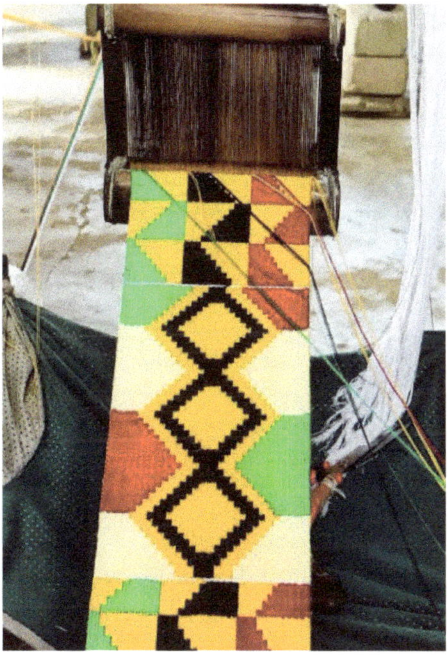

Kente cloth colors have special significance to the Asantes. The initial Kente cloths were in black and white only. With time yellow, black, red, and green became available from the bark of local trees. They are the traditional colors.

Yellow (made from *Dua Sika* Tree)

Black (made from *Dubuma* Tree)

Red (made from *Kasee* Tree)

Green (made from *Pobre* Tree)

Kente cloth colors and their significance.

Yellow	Preciousness, royalty, wealth, fertility
Pink	Feminine aspects of life, calmness, sweetness, and tenderness.
Red	Spiritual moods, bloodshed, sacrificial rites, strong political and spiritual feelings.
Maroon	Maternal association, healing, and protection from evil.
Blue	Holiness, peace, harmony, good fortune, and love.
Green	Vegetation, growth, and good health.

Gold	High status, preciousness, royalty, wealth, fertility.
White	Purity, healing, sanctification, and festive occasions
Black	Maturity, strong spiritual energy, and the spirits of the ancestors.
Grey	Ashes, healing, and spiritual cleansing.
Silver	Serenity, purity, and joy.
Purple	Feminine, earth, healing.

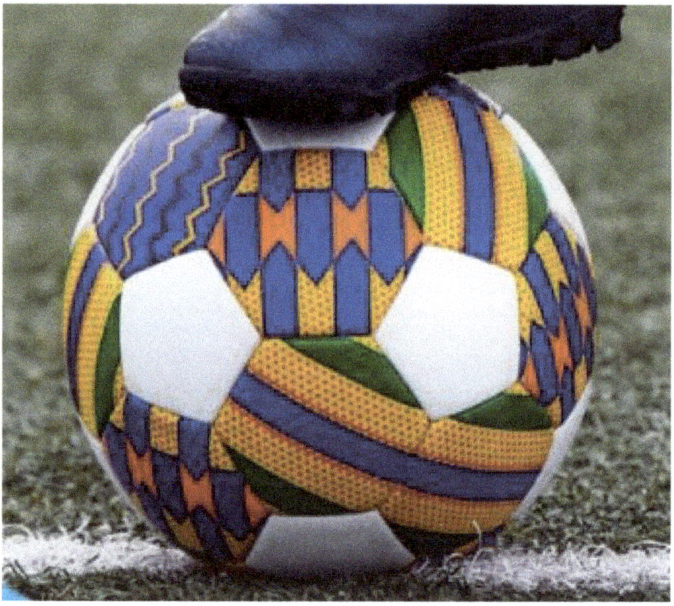

Ghana's pastime sport football (soccer)

Chapter 4

Kente Cloth Patterns

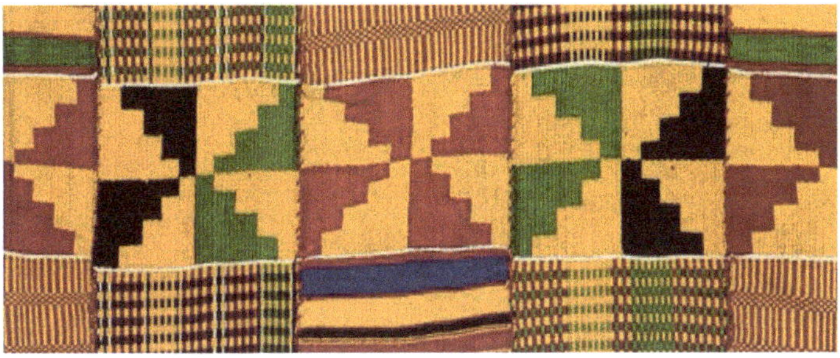

Kente cloth inlaid patterns or motifs also have special significance. The finished cloth does not derive its name only from these motifs but rather from the repeated motifs on the warp (the set of lengthwise yarns). Each strip has an open-end design that is followed by the main cloth design which is repeated several times and then a close-end design. The motifs feature geometric patterns, and each pattern has a specific meaning, relating to the history or beliefs of the Asantes. A master weaver must learn the meanings of all the patterns and how to create them.

There are five common patterns on the Kente cloth:

Square: The Kente with square patterns symbolizes creation and procreation and is therefore associated with femininity.

Cross: The Kente cloth with cross patterns symbolizes the breath of life.

Diamond: The Kente with diamond patterns symbolizes the duality of a monarch, as a King and as a human.

Triangle: The Kente with triangle patterns symbolizes the union of masculine and feminine principles to produce a third principle. It represents the life of a man, woman, and child. (The family)

Circle: The Kente with circle patterns represents infinity, no beginning or end. Eternal royalty.

Some of the most popular Kente motifs or patterns

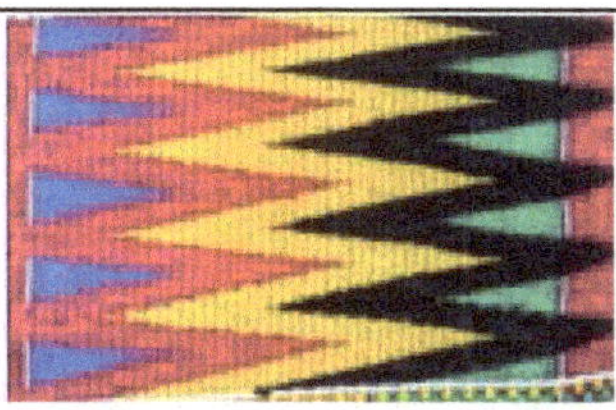	*Nkyinkyim* (Zigzag). Symbol of life not being straight path.
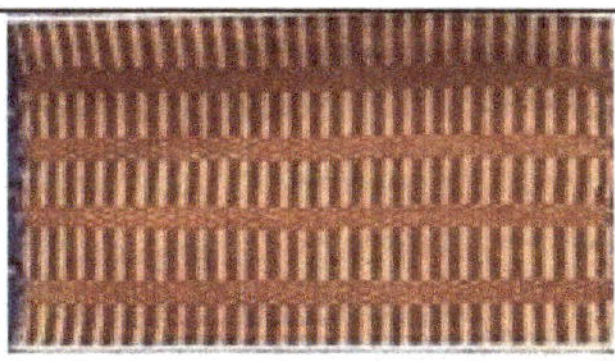	*Akyem* Shield Symbol of bravery
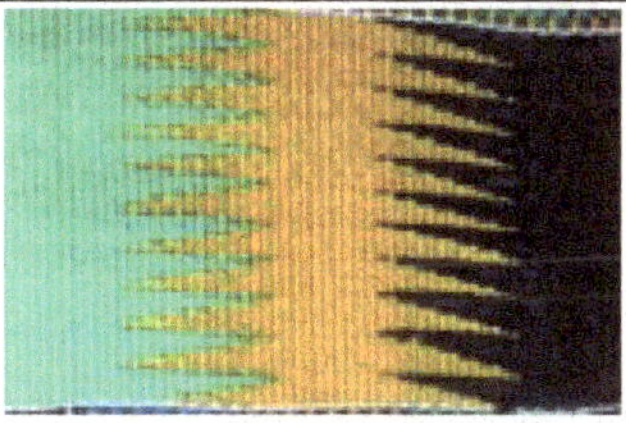	*Kwadum Asa* Empty gun powder keg or container.
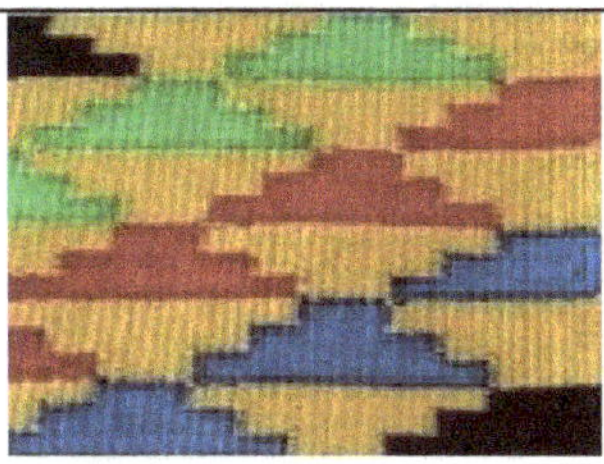	*Nsoroma* Stars Symbol of faithfulness and affection
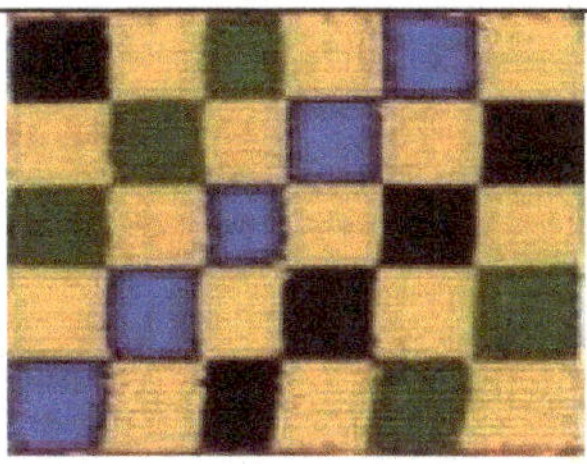	*Damedame* Checkerboard Symbol of wisdom, strategy, and intelligence)

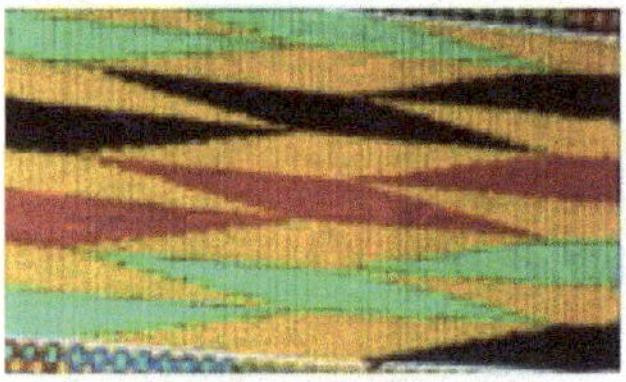	*Niata* Two-edged sword Symbol of good and bad
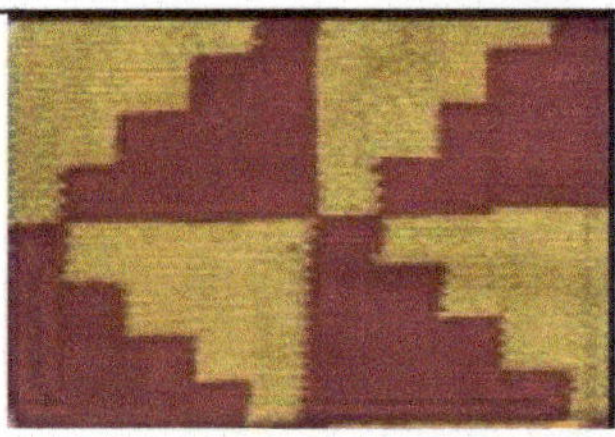	*Atwede* Steps Symbol of perseverance and advancement.
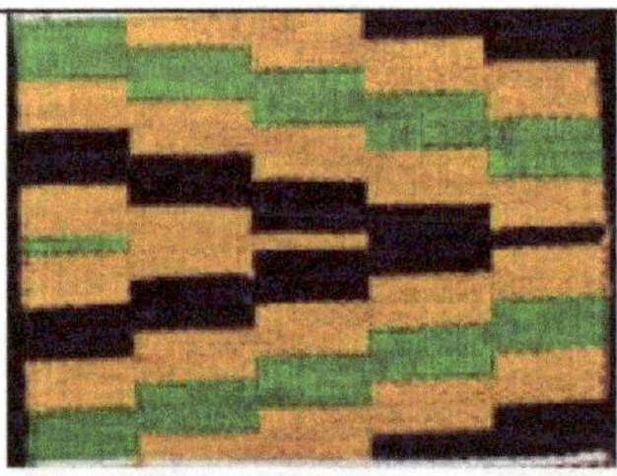	*Fa hia kotwere Agyeman (or Owuo Atwede – Death ladder)* Lay your poverty on Agyeman – 9th Asante King. A generous King.
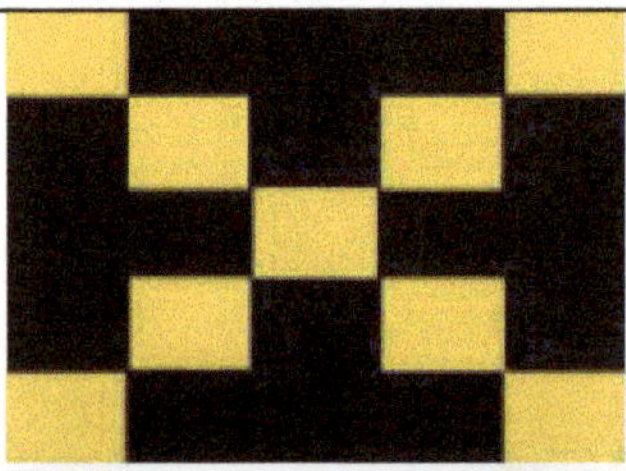	*Mpuankron* Nine tufts of hair. Symbol of democracy.
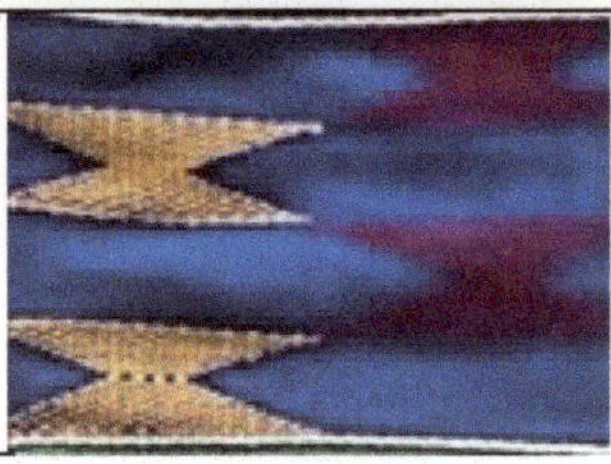	*Sika Adwa* Golden Stool Symbol of Soul of Asante Kingdom.

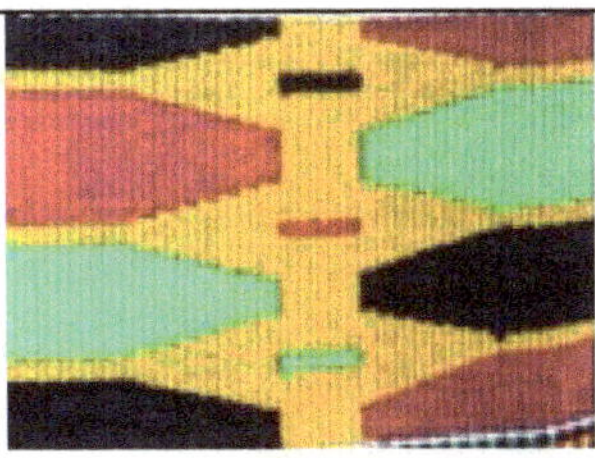	*Ohene Anewa* King's Eye Symbol of the King seeing everything.
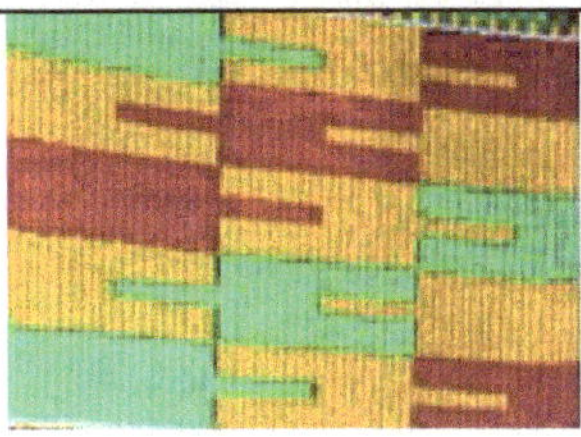	*Afa* I have taken it. Symbol of cooperation and efficiency.
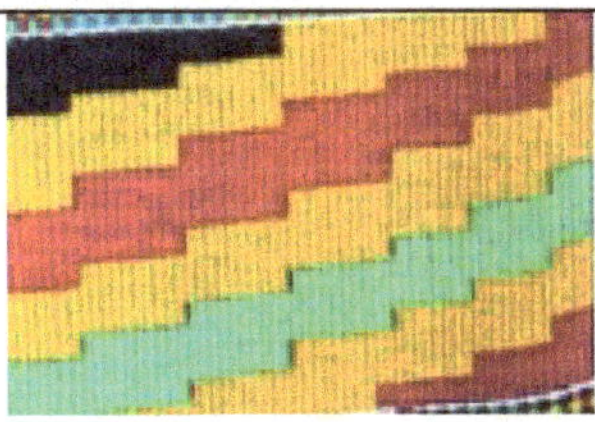	*Fatene* Go straight away.
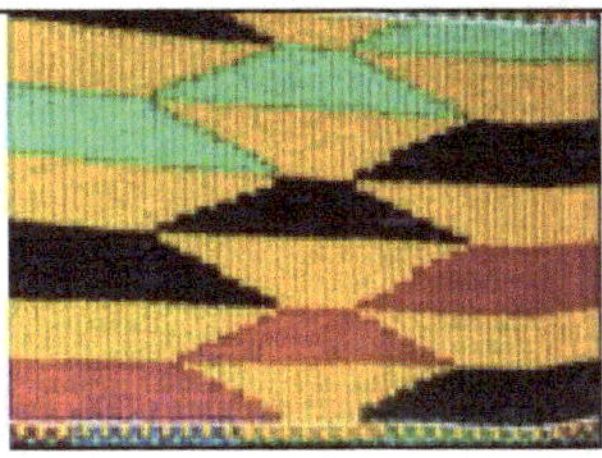	*Puduo* Pyramids Symbol of Practice, heritage, and continuity.
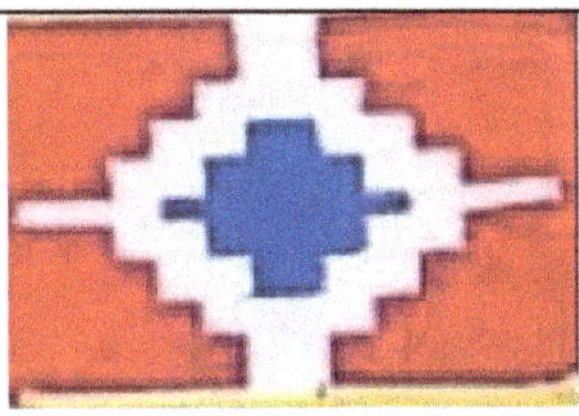	*Akoko Baata* Mother Hen Symbol of Motherliness or Tenderness.

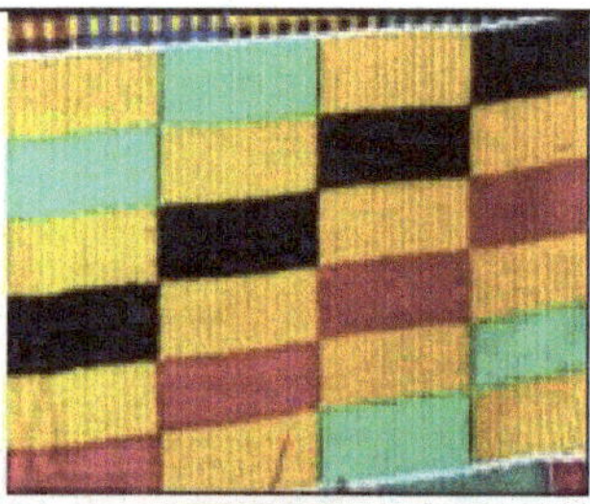	*Trom Nwoma* Droughts, Smooth weave.
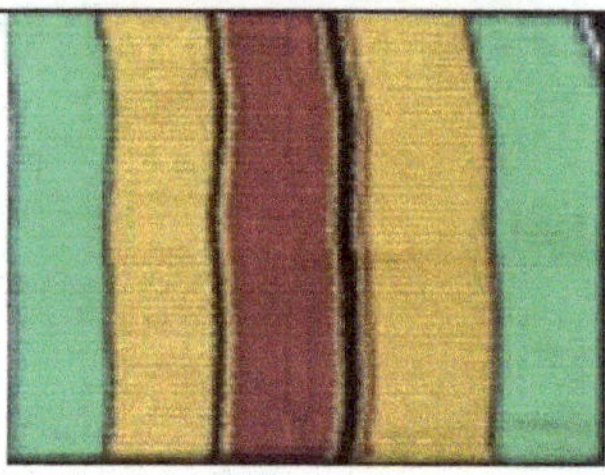	*Babadua* The Babadua tree is a Symbol of strength.
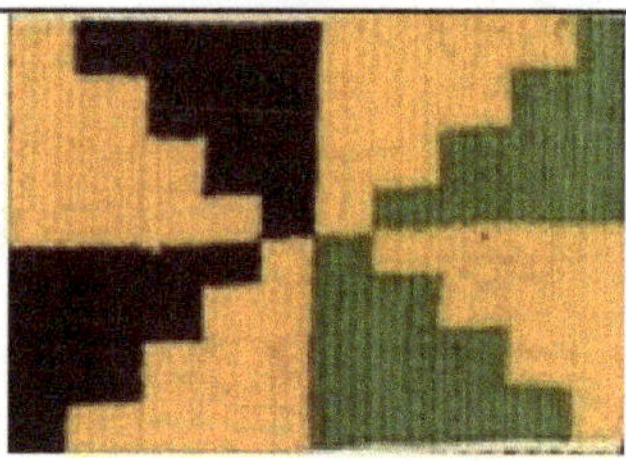	*Apremo* Lightning or thunder Symbol of Superior Military Strategy.
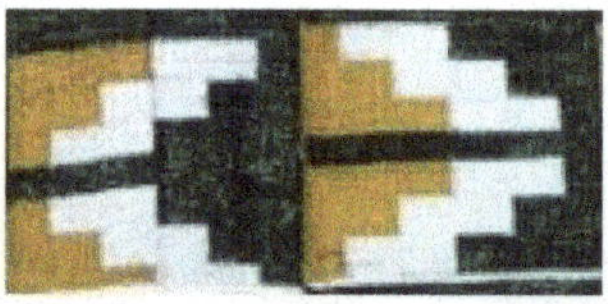	*Nanka Tire* Puff Adder's Head. Symbol of exploitation.
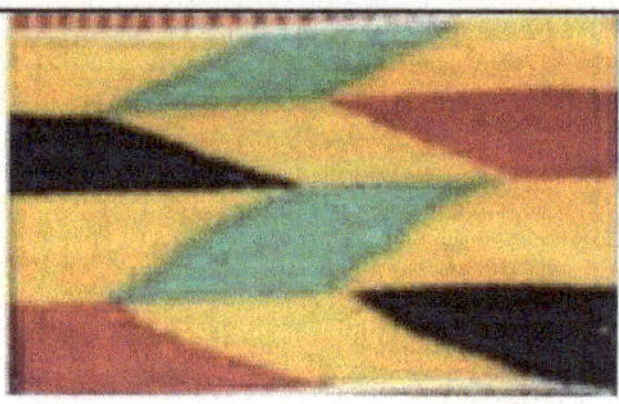	*Kyemfere* Potsherd Symbol of Knowledge.

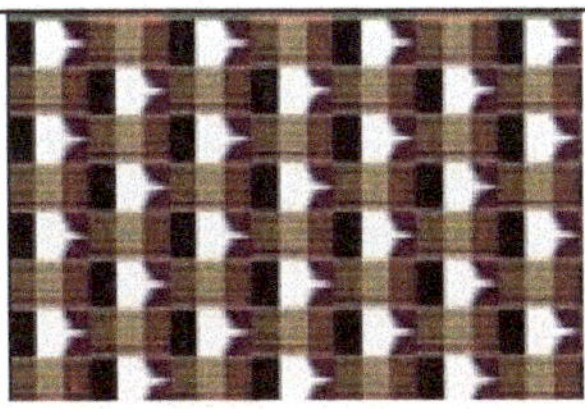	*Awia Repue* The rising Sun Symbol of Progress or renewal of energy.
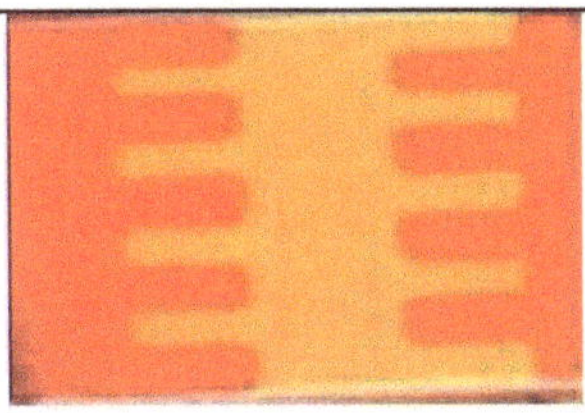	*Achimota Nsafoa* Achimota Keys Symbol of Knowledge.
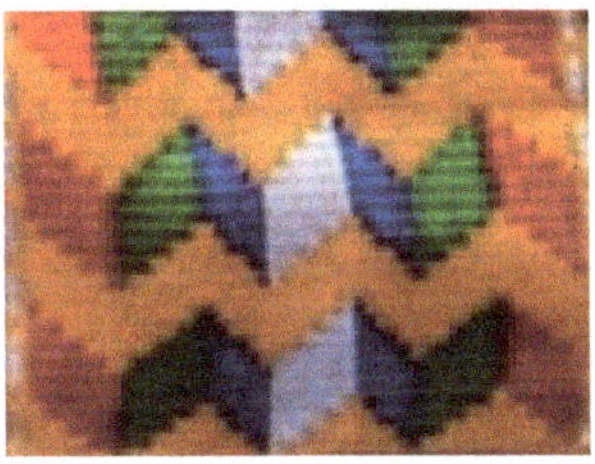	*Afafanto* Butterfly Symbol of tenderness, gracefulness, beauty, and calm.
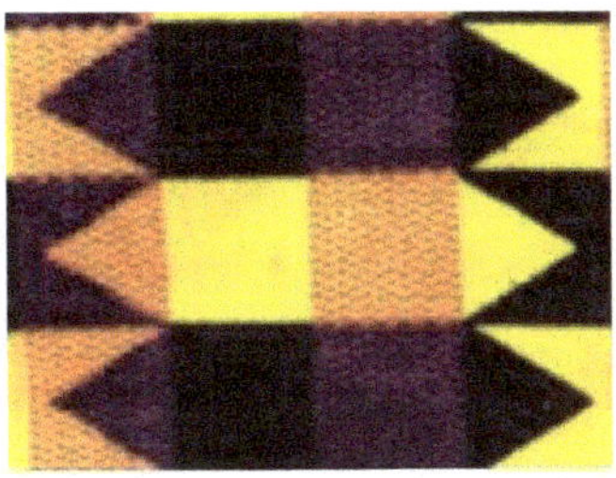	*Ntabon* Oars Symbol of unity, productivity, achievement, and progress.

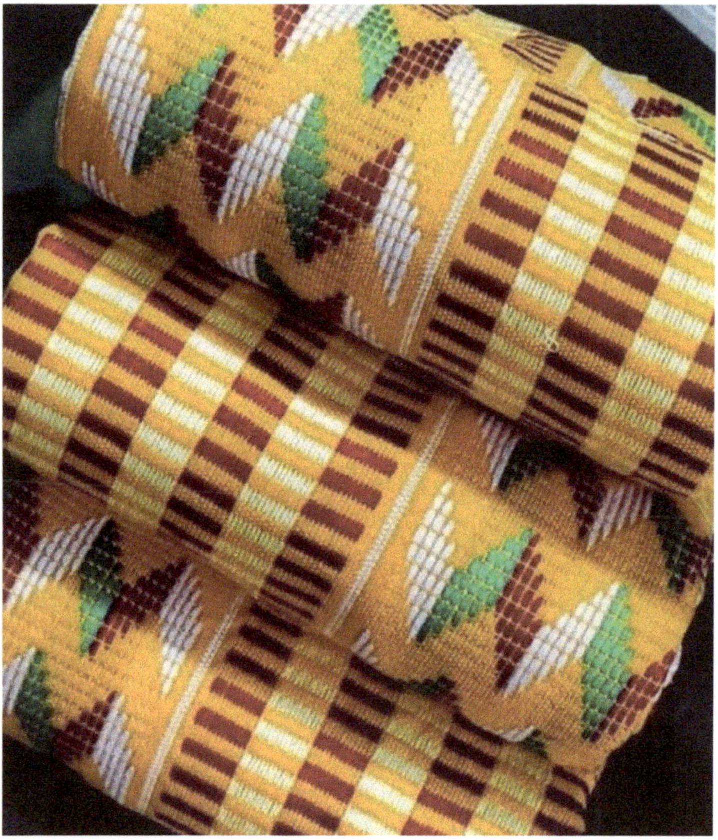

Afafanto (Butterfly) motif

Chapter 5

Kente Cloth Names - Traditional

Kente cloth names are normally based on situations and special events. The common criteria are Love (*Odo*), Riches (*Sika sem*), Hatred (*Otan*), Crisis (*Amani Ho*), Tradition (*Amanyo*), Proverbs (*Abako Sem*), Important People and special occasions. The weaver normally decides the Kente name but the first colored Kente was named by the then Asante King, Otumfuo Nana Prempeh I. Kente names used to be constant and easily recognized. That is not the case anymore. Modern weavers modify previous Kente designs slightly and give it a different name. There are two schools of thought about this phenomenon. One group is against it believing in maintaining the name the original weaver gave. Another group is in favor of it as it gives the modern generation the opportunity to redesign the old symbols and make them nicer. A few of the well know Kente have also been renamed after being used or presented to important persons. The renaming has been a big help to the sellers. All the renamed Kente have sold very well, according to Kente sellers.

Different Kente cloth may have some unique designs but the patterns in which the designs are used will guide you in knowing the name of the cloth. The name of the cloth as stated before is from the warp (threads that run along the length of the yardage up-and-down). The traditional Kente clothes are all done by weaving. Some contemporary Kente are made up of weaving and embroidery. There are also some which are stamped. (locally called *ntiamu*). All Kente have some weaving in them. The price of a Kente cloth depends on the amount of time and material used in the weaving. Most Kente last for a lifetime. It is not the case of "the higher the price the more durable it will be". You pay for the workmanship and not the durability. Except for the chiefs who prefer to change their Kente to suit the occasion it is not necessary to have a lot of different Kente.

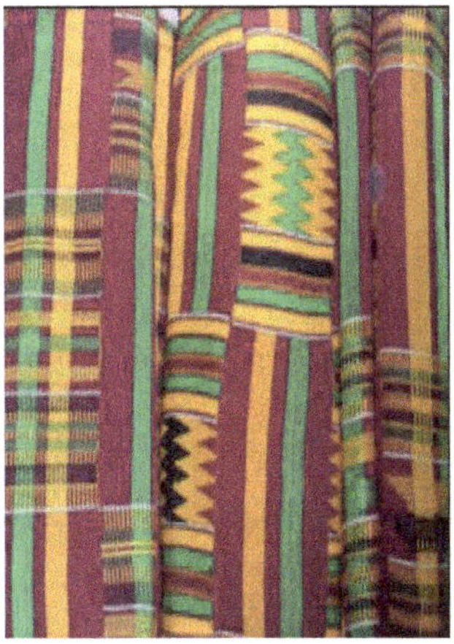

Oyoko Maa

Oyoko Maa means Oyoko women. This is the first colored Kente cloth woven by Ota Kraban. Oyoko is one of the eight (8) families (*Abusua)* in Ghana. When the cloth was presented to the Asantehene Otumfuo Nana Prempeh I (The King of the Asantes) by Nana Kwame Ketewa (Chief of Bonwire) and Ota Kraban (the weaver), he named it after the Oyoko women through whom the colored cloth came about hence the name *Oyoko maa.*

It became a royal cloth. In the past only the Asantehene could wear the Oyoko maa cloth. The reason being that no one was supposed to be dressed more beautifully than or like the Asantehene. A few prominent people who have been decorated or presented with the Oyoko maa Kente cloth are former US President Bill Clinton, Former world heavy weight boxing Champion Muhammed Ali.

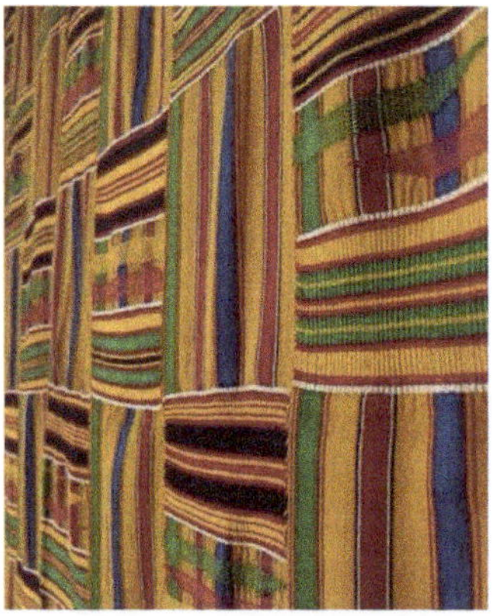

Sika Fre Mogya

Sika Fre Mogya means money attracts people. This is a popular Akan proverb. If you have money both your immediate family and other family members are drawn towards you all the time. People seek financial assistance from you and follow you wherever you go. The rich will always attract people for obvious reasons. This cloth was worn to the UN by Ghana's first President, Dr. Kwame Nkrumah.

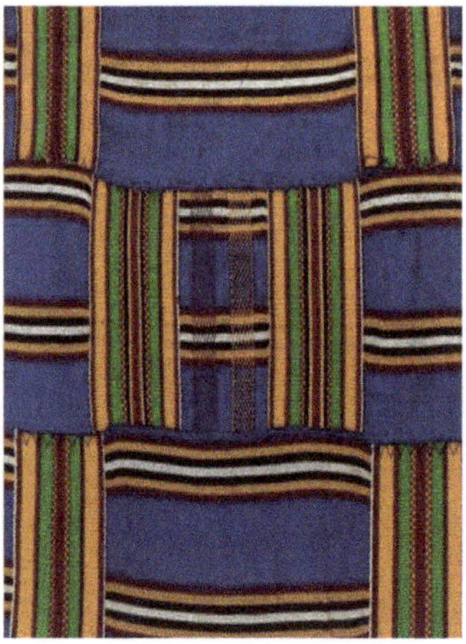

Emaa Da

Emaa Da means first of its kind. The history of this cloth is the blue color. Before this Kente, color blue was not available to the Kente weavers. They could only make color Kente using the traditional colors yellow, black, red, and green. They knew of the color and called it *Ewiam* (Sky) but could not make it. When they were finally able to make it, they did not spare it in this Kente. This was worn by Dr. Kwame Nkrumah upon his release from Prison.

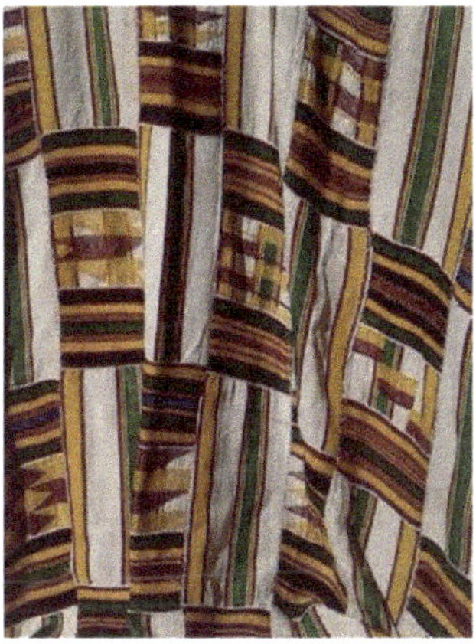

Toku Kra Toma

Toku kra Toma means Toku's Soul Cloth.

The cloth is named after the soul of a warrior Queen mother named Toku. She was defeated and beheaded in battle and was regarded as a courageous woman. In the past the cloth was worn by royalty during sacred ceremonies. The cloth symbolizes courageous leadership and heroic deeds. Legend has it that the weaver was told he will die upon completion of weaving that cloth. He therefore spent about 27 years to complete weaving it and died right after completion.

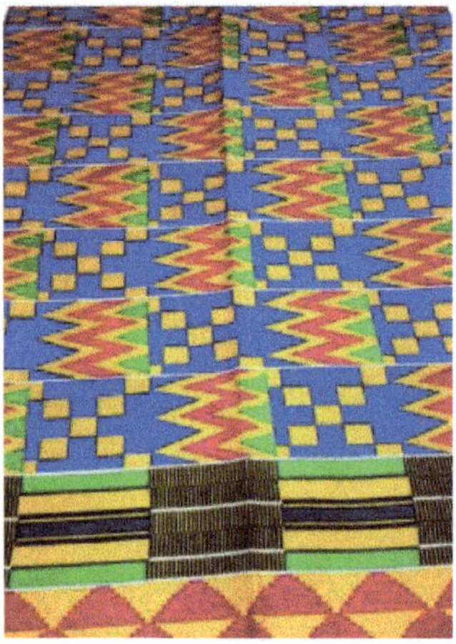

Fathia Fata Nkrumah

This Kente has two names. *Fathia Fata Nkrumah* (Fathia is suitable for Nkrumah) and *Obaakofo Mmu Man* (One person does not rule a nation).

It was named Fathia Fata Nkrumah when it was presented as a gift to the first President of Ghana Dr. Kwame Nkrumah and his wife, Fathia Nkrumah.

The Original name however is *Obaakofo Mmu Man*. It is based on the Akan system of participatory democracy. The nine yellow squares in a block called *Mpuankron*, represent nine tufts of hair. It was a ceremonial haircut of some royal functionaries who helped rulers make decisions. A few terms used for this Kente cloth are “one tree does not make a forest”, “one head cannot go into council”, “two heads are better than one”.

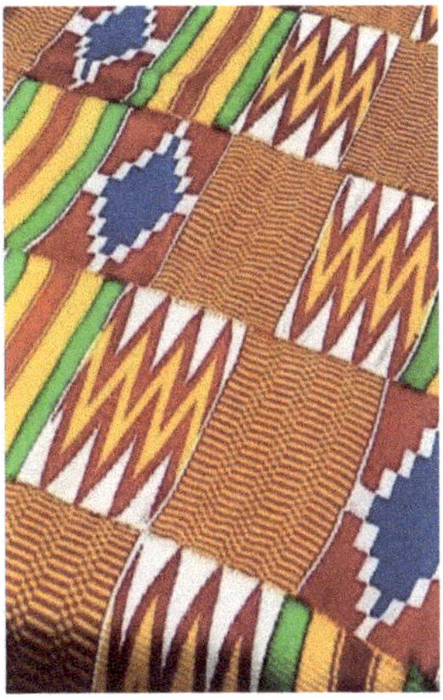

Wosene Woyonko A Otanwo

Wosene Woyonko A Otanwo means if you are better than your friend then he hates you. People sometimes confuse this design and that of *Fathia Fata Nkrumah*. The main difference is the nine (9) squares in the Fathia strip.

This Kente cloth was originally called *Ohene Abaduro,* meaning the King has returned. This was made in memory of the return of Asantehene Prempeh I upon his return from exile in the Seychelles in 1924. With some slight design modification, it was renamed *Wosene Woyonko A Otanwo.*

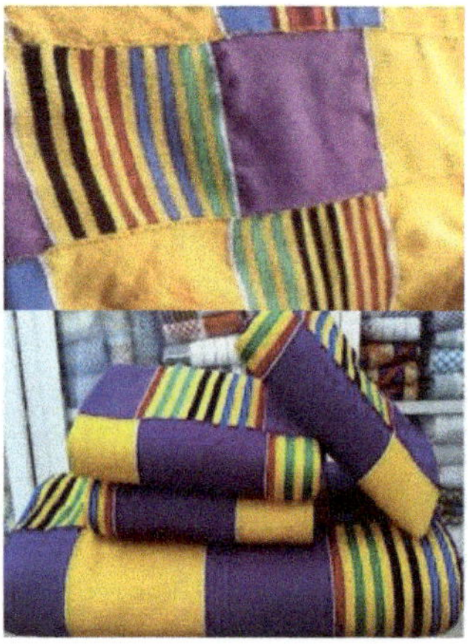

Nyame Akwan

This cloth *Nyame Akwan* means God's path or way. The symbolism of this is that God has many paths. When one door closes another will open. It is to encourage each other especially when things are not going well. The top picture is an older version, and the bottom picture is a more recent version. It comes in many different shades, but the purple and yellow combination seems to dominate.

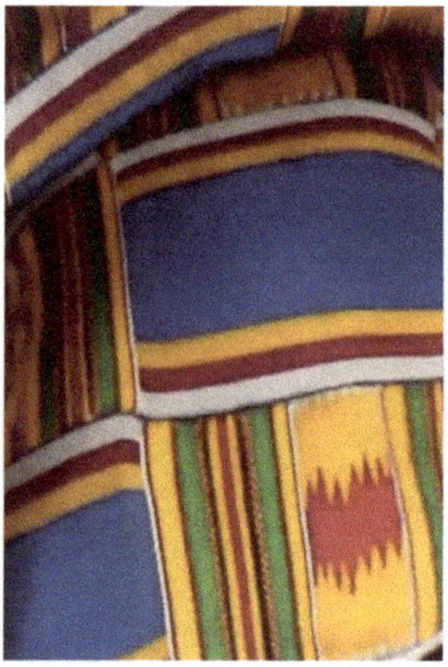

Obi Nkye Obi Kwanmusi

This traditional Kente called *Obi Nkye Obi Kwanmusi* translates to "it does not take long for one to offend the other". The common phrase for this is "To Err is human, to forgive is divine". The rational for this name is that we must learn to forgive each other since we are likely to offend others sooner than we think.

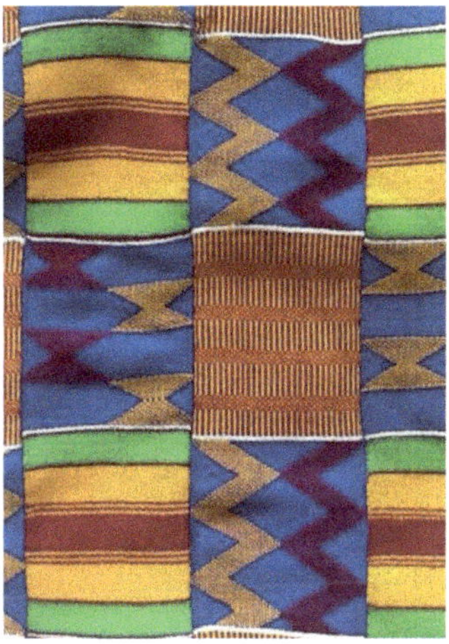

Abusua Ye Dom

Abusua Ye Dom means the extended family is a force. This cloth name symbolizes strong family bond. This cloth was made when two factions of the same Oyoko family were fighting to nominate the next Asante King. Eventually Prempeh I was enstooled at age 18 in 1888. The other faction fled the Kingdom, most to Cote d'Ivoire (formally Ivory Coast).

The motifs used here are *Babadua* (yellow, green, and red lines), The Shield (*Akyem*), Golden Stool (*Sika Dwa*) and Zigzag *(Nkyinkyim).*

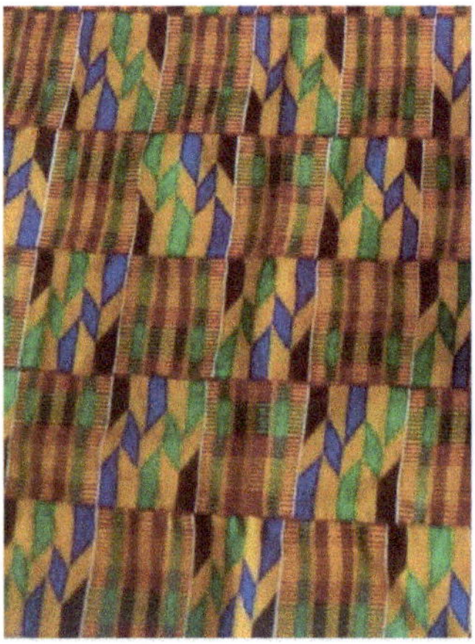

Edwin Asa

Edwin Asa means all design motifs are used up. Legend has it that a weaver wanted to create a Kente that was unique. After using all the motifs known to the weavers at that time, he came up with this beautiful cloth and named it *Edwin Asa* (All motifs are finished). The true meaning though is the design is complete, not finished. It takes more time and raw materials than a standard Kente cloth. This cloth symbolizes royalty, elegance and superior craftmanship.

The name is not derived from the designs but from the fact that each block along the whole length has a design in it. Any design combinations can be used to make *Edwin Asa*. This one used the *Nsatea* motif.

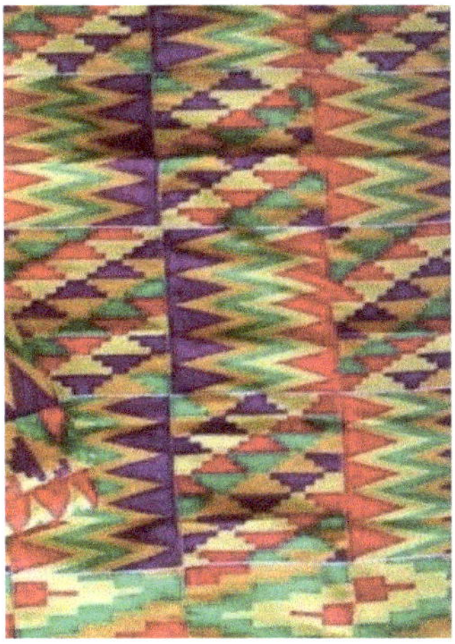

Edwin-Si-Edwin-So

"Edwin Si Edwin So" means one main cloth design after another. This cloth has the zigzag design alternating the stars design. There is no block without a design. It is one of most time-consuming and expensive cloths. Only the rich could afford it and was originally named *Wabo bra* meaning "You have made it in life".

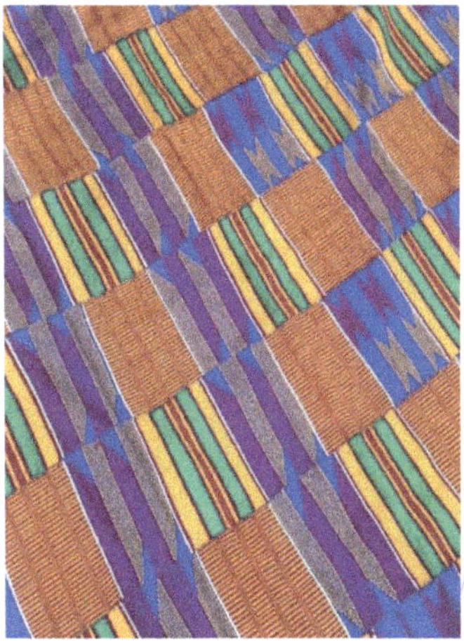

Ohene Afro Hyen

This Kente called *Ohene Afro Hyen* means the King has boarded a ship. The cloth was named in commemoration of the Asante King Agyeman Prempeh II's trip to England in 1937. Some of the motifs used in the warp design are the *Babadua* (yellow, green and red lines), The Shield (*Akyem*), Golden Stool (*Sika Dwa*) and broken pot (*kyemfre*).

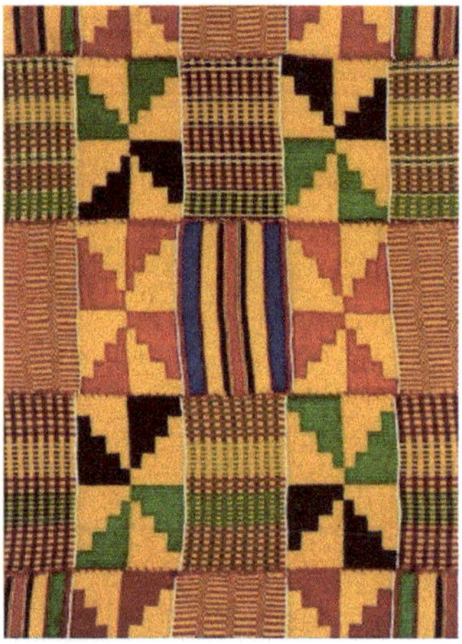

Apremo Ato

Apremo Ato means the Apremo Gun has fired. This was the period when the British fought the Asantes in the Yaa Asantewaa war (or the Golden Stool war). In those days, the British had a big gun called *Premo* which the Asantes called "*Apremoo*". This gun was Italian made. The British used to fire this gun at 12 noon each day to remind the Asantes that they were still around. Any time it was fired the response was *Apremo Ato* meaning Apremo has fired. It tells time.

The British at that time were demanding the surrender of the famous Golden Stool from the Asantes.

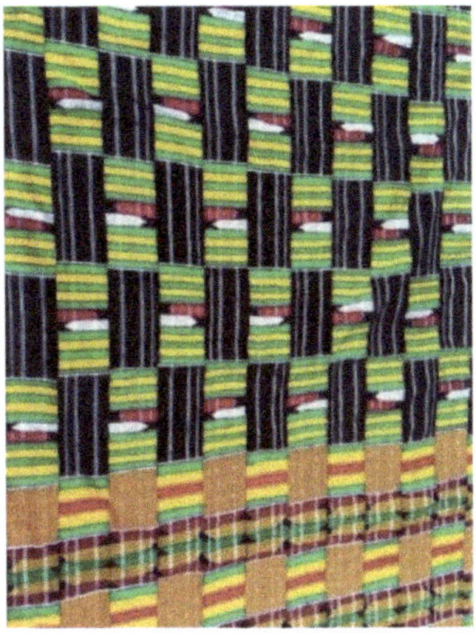

Kyeretwie

Kyeretwie means Leopard catcher. It commemorates an incident during the reign of the Asante King Kwaku Dua (1838 -1867) who tested the courage of his warriors by ordering them to catch a live leopard.

The black vertical warp stripes represent the black spots (rosettes) in a leopard's fur. In the past, the cloth was worn only by the Asantehene or by other chiefs with his permission. This cloth symbolizes bravery and courage.

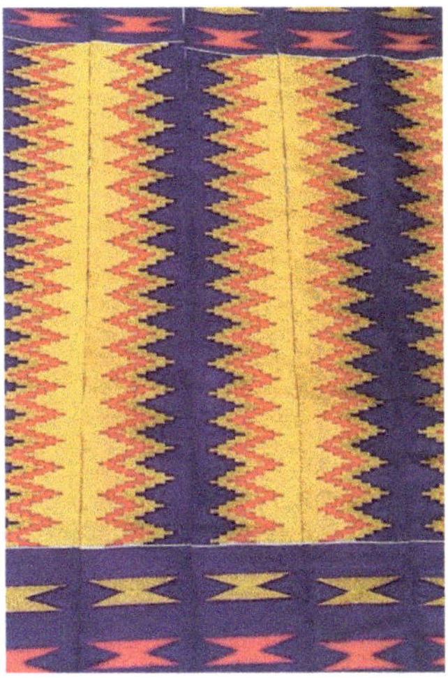

Nanka Tire

Nanka Tire means Puff Adder's head. The symbolism of this cloth is exploitation. This is related to an old Akan proverb which says, "I cannot even carry the Python, yet you ask me to use the Puff

Adder's head as the carrying pad". "*Meso annini mentumi, wose menfa nanka tre mmo kahyire*". The open and close ends in this cloth used the Golden stool design.

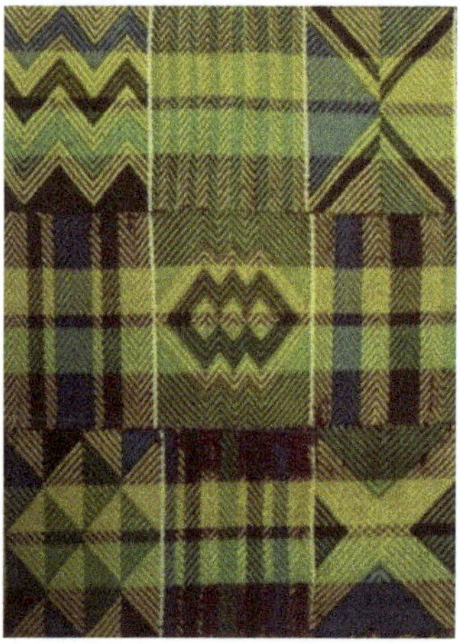

Asasia

Asasia means "Very Rare" It is one of the premier Kente cloths. It was the exclusive preserve of the King of the Asantes. It could only be woven or used with the explicit permission or consent of the Asantehene.

As noted in the history chapter, there are only a handful of people in the world who have the expertise to weave the Asasia Kente. It requires about three sets of design heddles to weave the Asasia Kente.

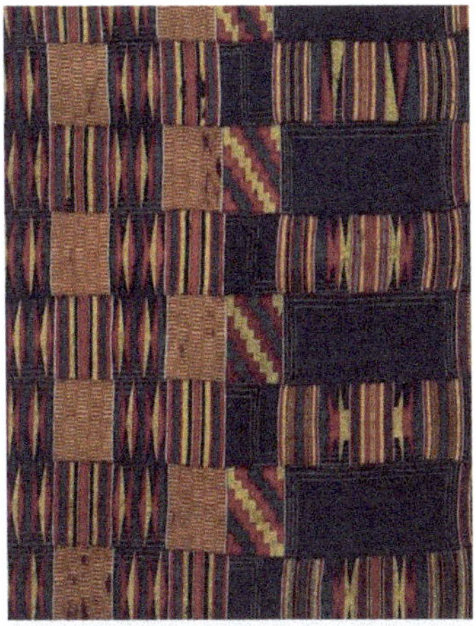

Nkontompo

Nkontompo means "Lies". The weaving of this cloth is also limited to very few master weavers from Bonwire. It is used by the wearers to tell their side of a story without speaking. When there is a case between two litigants and one of them wears the Nkontompo Kente, it symbolizes that the other party is not telling the truth.

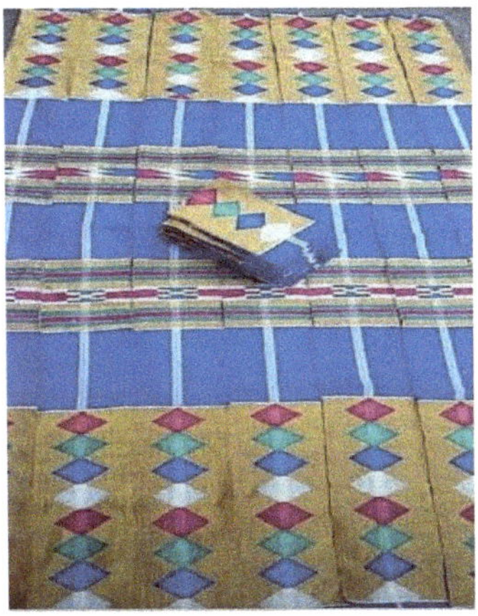

Denkyembuor

Denkyembuor means "Crocodile Stone". Crocodile stone refers to diamonds. Legend has it that crocodiles are the protectors of diamonds in a river. They are found in the very deep part of the river.

Parts of the river with diamond deposits are believed to always have huge crocodiles protecting it. To get to the diamonds one must get rid of the crocodile.

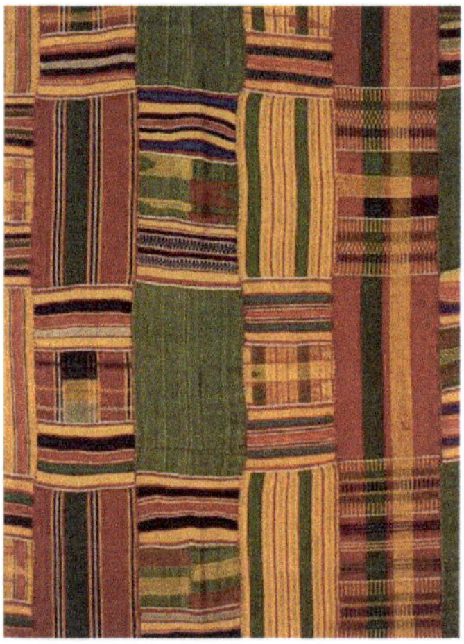

Dakoro Yesre

Dakoro Yesre means one day is for laughter. The symbolism of this cloth is that every difficult moment is interspersed with a day of reprieve.

There is no period in anyone's life that all the days will be gloomy.

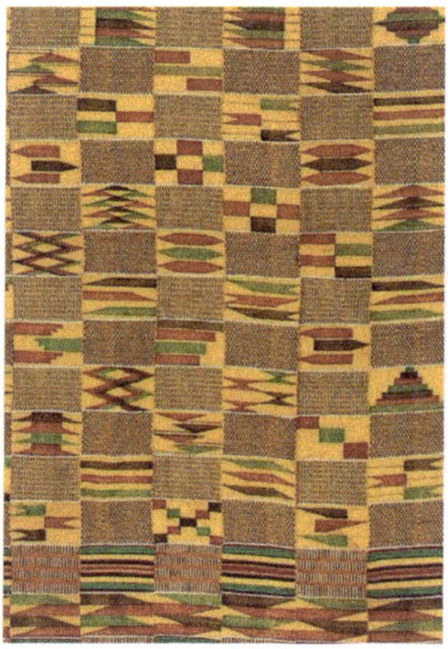

Sika Futuro

Sika Futuro means Gold Dust. This cloth was so named because the cloth design resembled the gold dust that was used as money in those days. It symbolizes wealth and prosperity.

Chapter 6

Kente Cloth Names - Contemporary

Kente cloth names used to be quite easy to ascertain. With time weavers wanted to be adventurous so the race to create new designs started. We now have over three hundred (300) Kente designs and most of them are a slight variation of the traditional designs. A lot of the new Kente designs do not really have names. We also now have cloth that are not fully Kente. They are a combination of Kente and other contemporary materials. Whatever the innovation is, it starts with Kente as the base.

The *Akunee Ntoma* came about when weavers intelligently added embroidery to Kente weaving. The popular name for it now is Obama Kente because that was the type of Kente cloth presented to the 44th US President Barack Obama when he visited Ghana in the year 2009. It is basically, a single weave Kente cloth with Embroidery added. Most of the Embroidery are the Adinkra symbols but technically any artwork can be used. This Kente cloth is probably more popular now than most of the traditional Kente because of its beauty. It also gives the wearer a false sense of looking like a King. A version was even created for the Asante King and named Otumfuo Obama Kente.

Another version of Kente also known as *Ntiamu* has been introduced. Ntiamu simply means stamping a design into the cloth. In this version the single weave Kente cloth is stamped with any of the numerous Adinkra symbols or any other artwork the weaver or buyer requires. This type of Kente did not originate from Bonwire. It is the ingenuity of people from Ntonso, another town in the Kwabre East Area of Ashanti Region, Ghana. The Ntonso people are renowned for its Adinkra crafts. The weavers from Bonwire know how to create this version of Kente but it is fair to give credit to the people who invented it. Since this is not from Bonwire this book will not go into details on the creation of the stamped Kente.

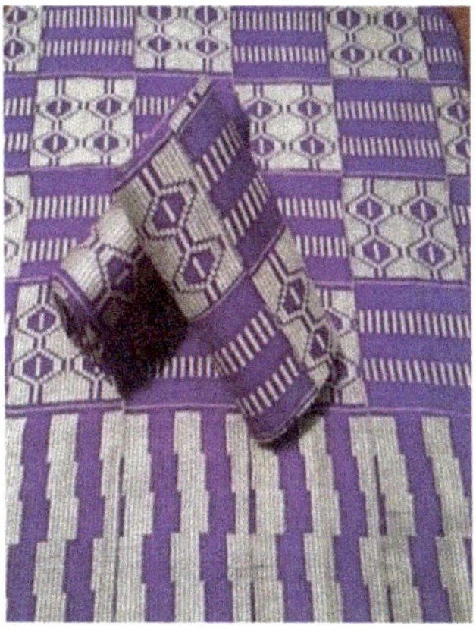

Makoma So Ade

Makoma so Ade means "My heart desire". The design of this Kente is all about love. The purple color is associated with feminine aspects of life. The weaver decided that name because the cloth was very dear to him. The design is quite simple making the cost affordable for the average person.

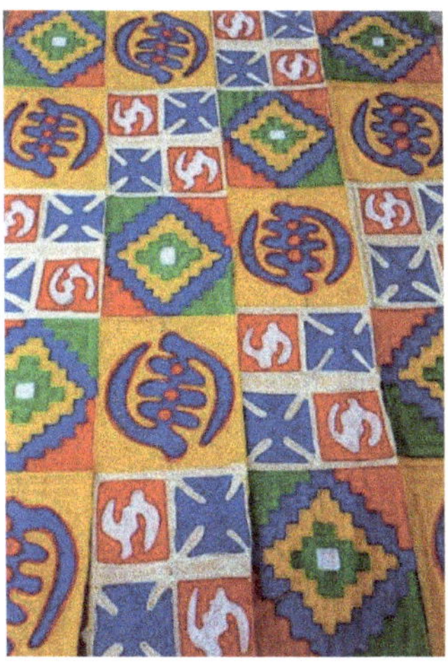

Obama

Obama Kente is so named because it was presented to President Obama, the 44th US President when he visited Ghana. It is a single weave Kente and embroidery. The symbols are all embroidery.

The embroidery is normally one of the Adinkra symbols, but it can be any artwork. Another name is

Akunee Ntoma which is meant for people of high social standing. This is a Kente with multiple names.

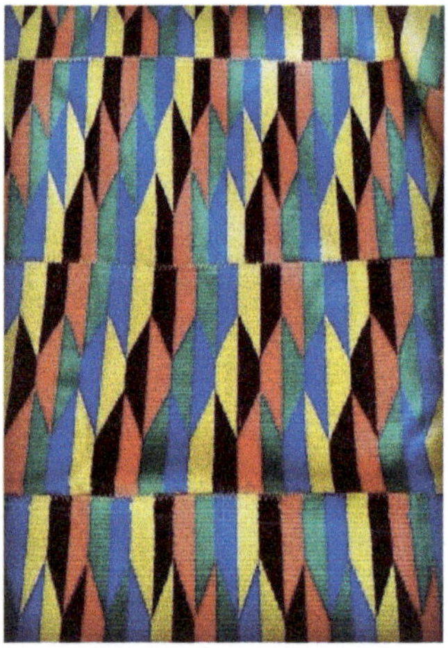

Nsatea

This Kente is called "*Nsatea Nyinaa Enye Pe*" meaning all the fingers are not equal. The short name is *Nsatea.*

The symbolism of this cloth is that we are not all going to be equal, everyone is unique. People are born short, average, and tall. Some people are going to be rich, some not so rich and others poor. Some are going to be smart and others not too smart.

Whatever your situation you must realize that everyone is unique.

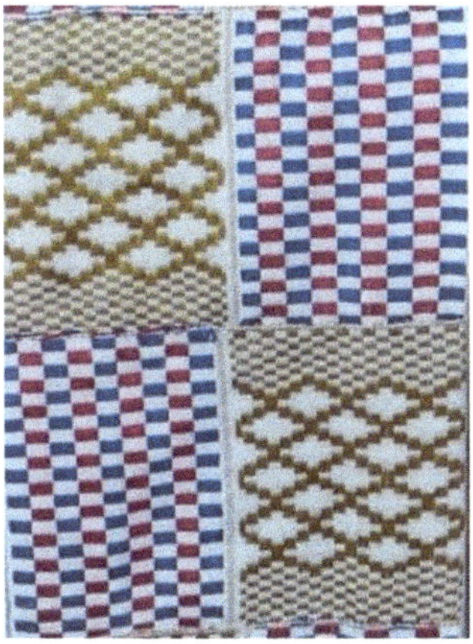

Mrepa Wo Wanim

"Mrepa Wo Wanim" means better days are ahead of you. It is extremely popular mainly due to its name.

Apart from its beauty it gives hope to people especially in times of difficulties. It is also not made up of too many designs and will not be too time consuming to make a single strip. That means it will be affordable for most people.

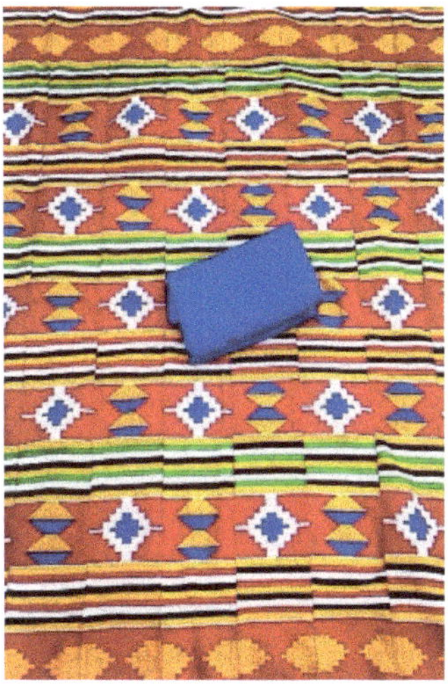

Akoko Baatan

Akoko Baatan means "Mother Hen". You will notice the main design from the motifs section in chapter four. A mother hen is very protective of its young. The protection a mother gives the children is something to be thankful everywhere. The cloth is a thank you to mothers. The cloth symbolizes Motherliness and tenderness.

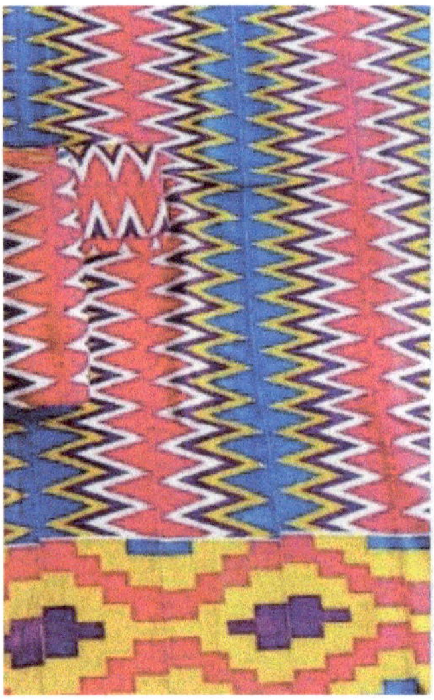

Nkyinkyim

Nkyinkyim means "Zigzag". It symbolizes the path of life. It is not a straight path for anyone. There are twists and turns in everybody's life. This is a simple design to make the cloth affordable. The open-end and close-end of this cloth used the *Nanka tre* motif. *Nanka Tre* is the Puff Adder's head. It symbolizes exploitation. The situation of being overburden with work.

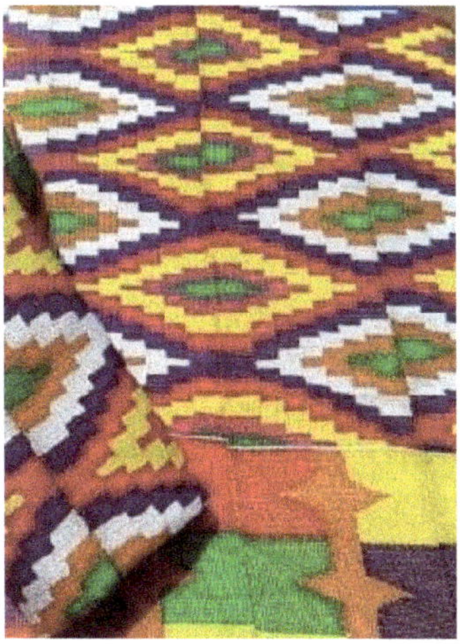

Ahwenepa Nkasa

Another Kente cloth about love. *Ahwenepa Nkasa* means the good waist beads does not make noise. A good wife does not give you problems, very polite and a blessing from God. There are so many ways to describe a good wife, but they all point to the fact that a good wife is a blessing to both husband and children.

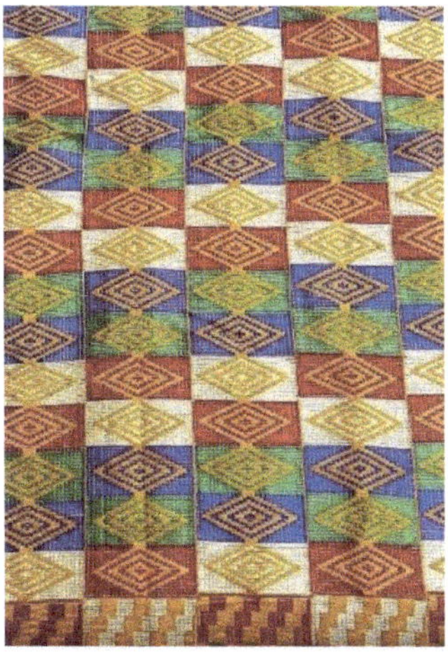

Odo Ntentan

Odo Ntentan means web of love. The design is just like the spider web. It is for lovers and it displays how the lovers web is used to catch lovers.

The open-end and close-end design for this cloth used the *Fatene pattern.*

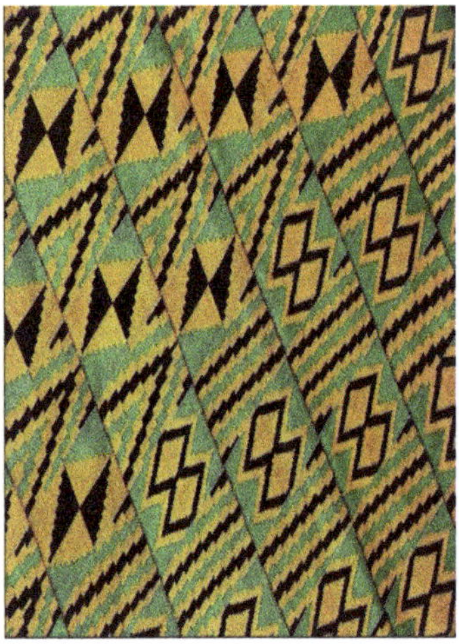

Clinton Kente

Clinton Kente was named after it was presented as a gift to President Bill Clinton, the 42nd president of the United States from 1993 to 2001.

It was wrapped around President Bill Clinton in a rally on March 23, 1998 in Accra by the then president of Ghana Flt. Lt. Jerry John Rawlings. The name is not based on the design but the personality.

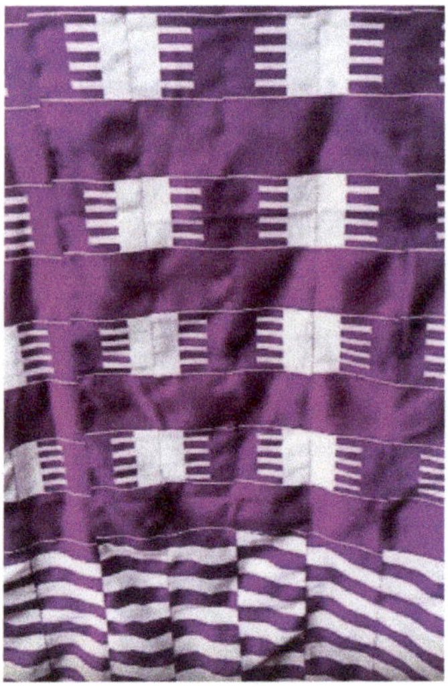

Achimota Nsafoa

Achimota Nsafoa means Achimota Keys. Achimota *is* one of the more prestigious premier high schools established in Ghana. Very few people at that time the symbol was made could be admitted to the school.

The key to Achimota school represents the key to achieving a higher educational knowledge and thus a high social standing in Ghana.

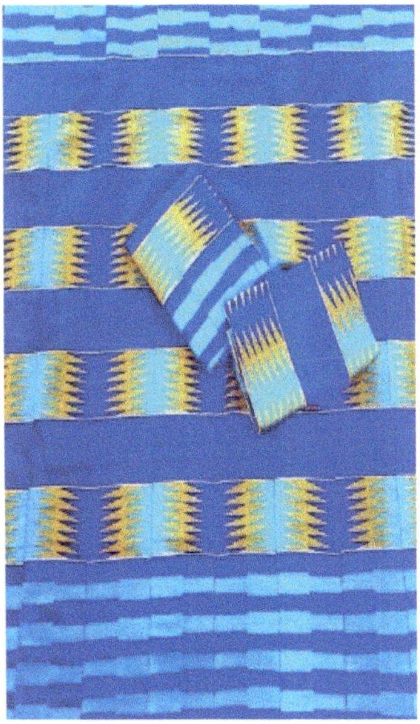

Kwadum Asa

The Kwadum Asa Kente is simply using the Kwadum Asa motif to weave the cloth. Kwadum Asa is the symbol for an empty gun powder keg. This is a simple design used to make the cloth affordable.

Guns and gun powder had been part of the Asantes during the period of many wars. An empty gun powder keg is not something to have in the war field.

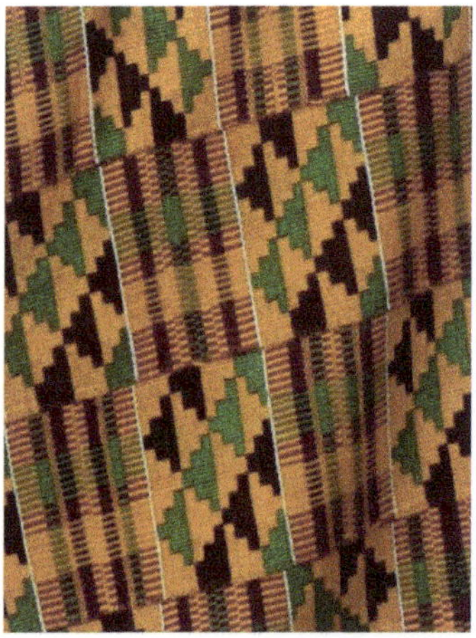

Nsoronma

Nsoronma means star. The design is a representation of stars. The stars and the moon were the main source of light in the night before electricity became available. The star is a symbol of faithfulness and affection in the Asante culture. It symbolizes feminine aspects of the Asante life.

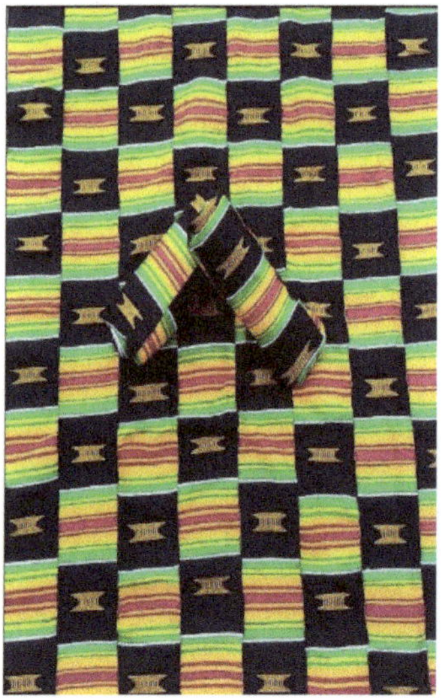

Sika Adwa

Sika Adwa means the Golden Stool. This refers to the famous Golden Stool that was believed to have descended from the sky.

It was a gift from the great spiritual leader Okomfo Anokye to the first Asante King Osei Tutu I. The Asantes believe their existence is linked to the Golden stool and that if the stool is captured it will mean the end of the Asante kingdom. This cloth was made to commemorate the Golden Stool.

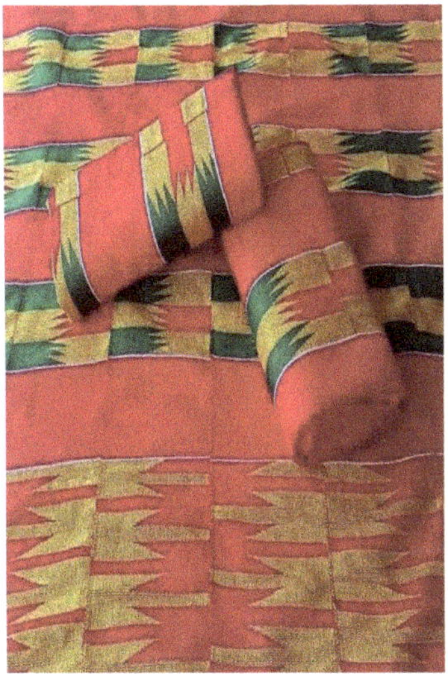

Nnua Ntoma

"Nnua Ntoma" means sibling cloth. Siblings are the smallest units of family system. The Asantes practiced the extended family system, where a family could be a whole village.

The sibling bond is however the most intimate. The design is depicting the closeness of one to his or her siblings. It is a sign of unity that exists among siblings.

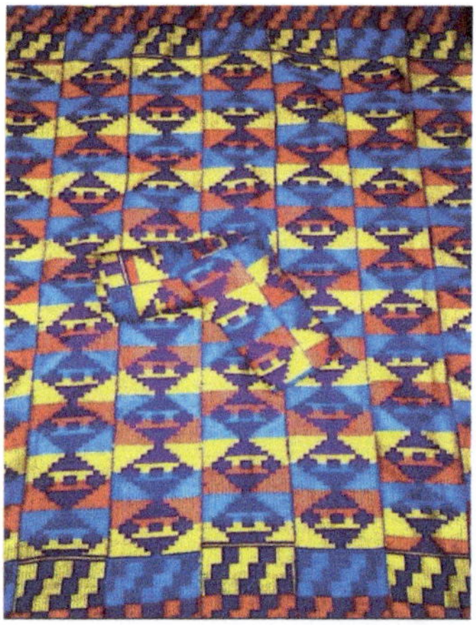

Free Education

Free education Kente is very recent. It commemorates the policy of the government of Ghana in September 2019 to make the senior high school education free to all Ghanaians. The main motif in this cloth is the school building. There are various colors, and different styles for this cloth. The design for the weft is the *Fatene*.

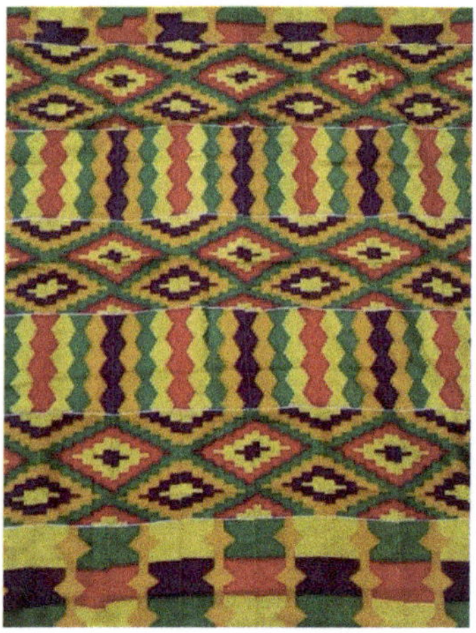

Gifty Anti

Gifty Anti is a Ghanaian journalist and broadcaster. This Kente was not made for her but she made it exceedingly popular by using it together with her husband (Nana Ansah Kwao IV) for their wedding.

Normally one will have called this Kente *Edwin-si-Edwin so*. (one main cloth design after another) The new name now is Gifty Anti.

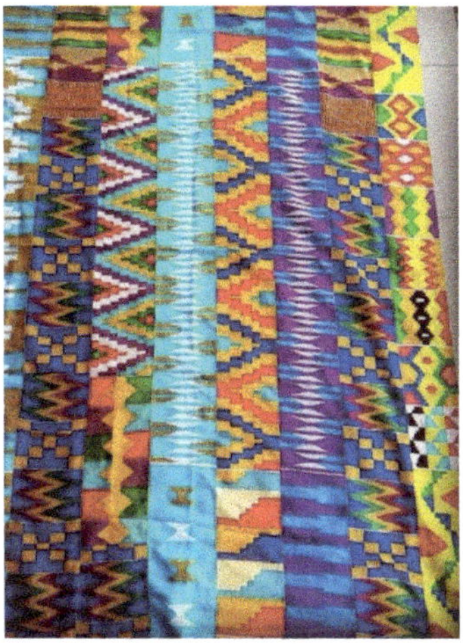

Nsasawa

"Nsasawa" means mixture. The weaver sometimes happens to have a lot of leftovers from previous orders. He then puts them together to get this unique cloth called *Nsasawa*.

Nsasawa are not always just leftovers. Sometimes, they are intentionally used to create extremely attractive designs. *Nsasawa* can be from two to as many different designs as needed to make the cloth. Though attractive and beautiful, people prefer a Kente cloth that has a unique name to *Nsasawa*.

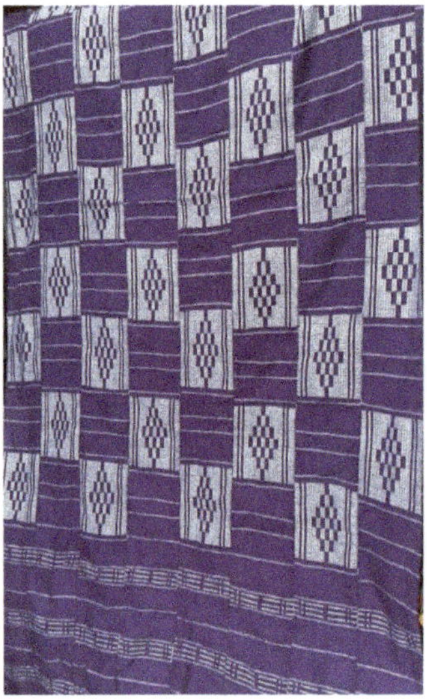

Theresa Kufuor

Theresa Kufuor Kente was created to honor the wife of the President of Ghana at that time President John Agyekum Kufuor (President 2001 – 2009)

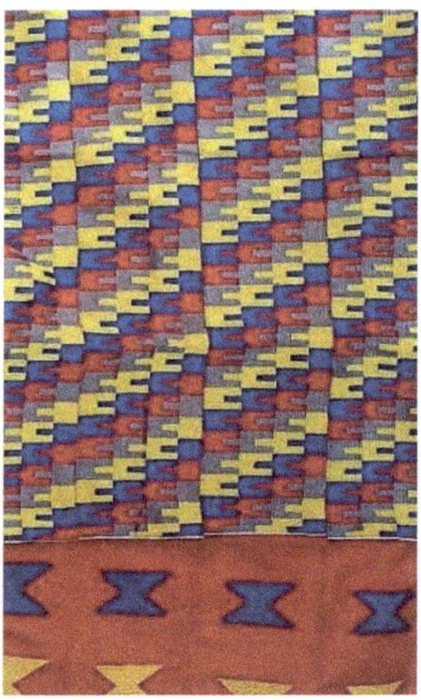

Afa Kente

Afa means I have taken it. This is a symbol of cooperation and efficiency. The Afa was a device for smelting raw gold or iron. The design resembles a fork without the center teeth.

Chapter 7

Kente Cloth – Adinkra Symbols

The two types of Kente that use the Adinkra Symbols are the *Akunee* Kente (Obama Kente) and the *Ntiamu* Kente. The Obama Kente discussed earlier is a single weave Kente with the embroidery of mostly Adinkra Symbols or any other artwork. Below are sample Obama Kente (Kente and Embroidery).

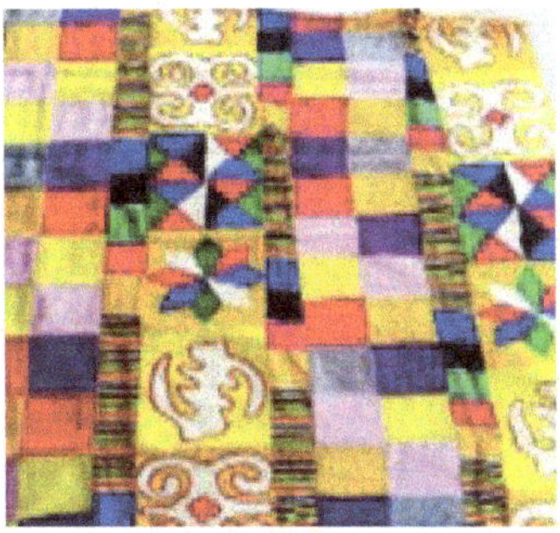

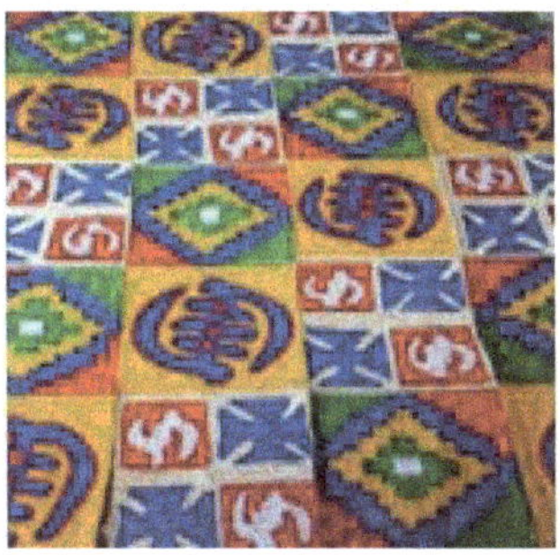

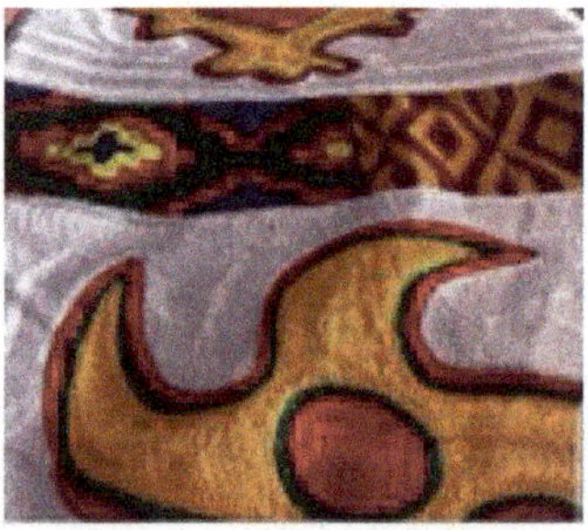

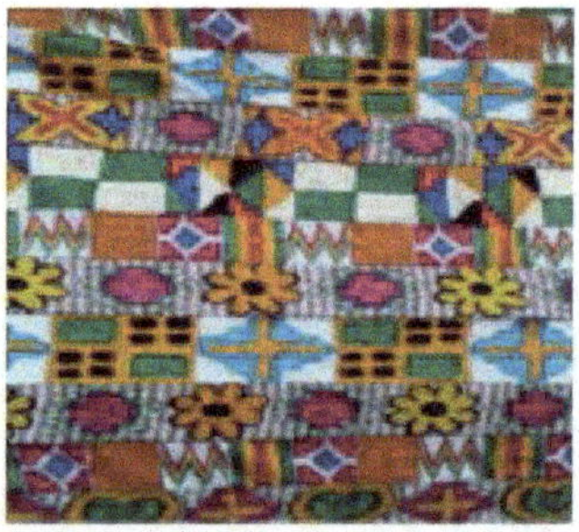

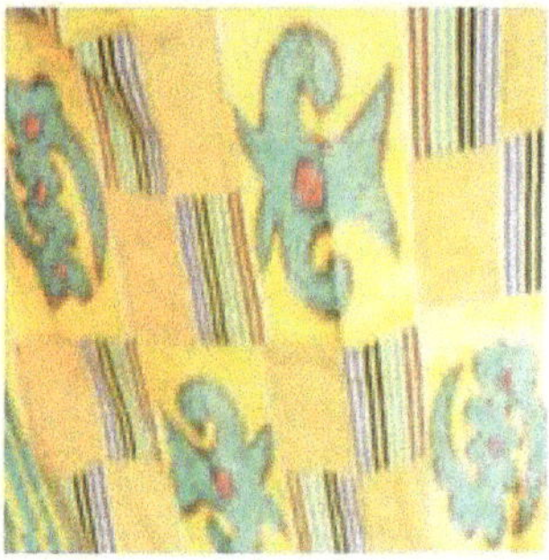

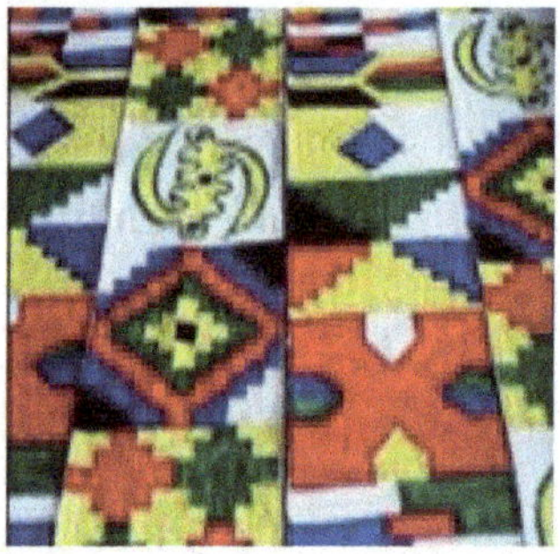

Adinkra symbols are also Asante historical and philosophic symbols. They were originally printed on cloth for Asante royals. They have been part of the Ghanaian culture since time immemorial. Their use in Kente weaving is however recent. Below are some well-known Adinkra Symbols and their meanings.

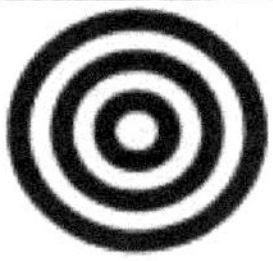 ***Adinkrahen*** King of Adinkra Symbols Leadership and charisma.	 ***Akoben*** War horn Vigilance and wariness
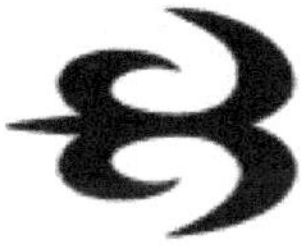 ***Akoko Nan*** Leg of a hen Nurturing and discipline	 ***Akoma*** Heart Patients and tolerance
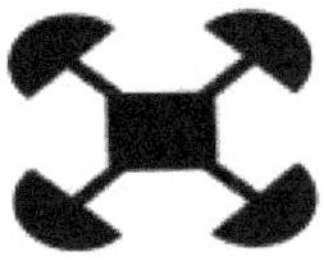 ***Akoma Ntoaso*** Heart Extension Agreement, understanding	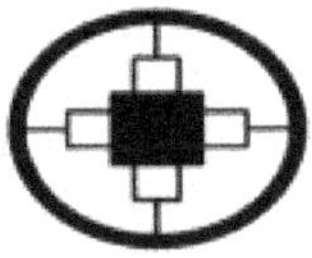 ***Dame Dame*** Checkerboard Wisdom, intelligence

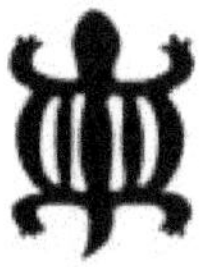 ***Denkyem*** Crocodile Adaptability, cleverness	 ***DwanniMmen*** Ram's Horns Strength and humility
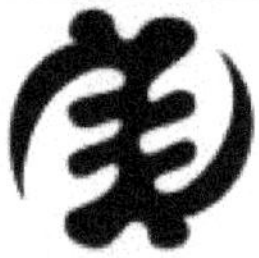 ***Gye Nyame*** Except God Supremacy of God.	 ***Funtumfunafu*** Siamese Crocodile Unity, common destiny
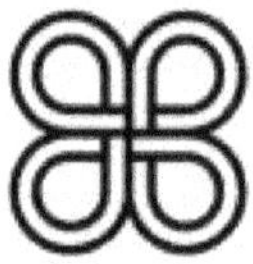 ***Mpatapo*** Knot of reconciliation Peacemaking.	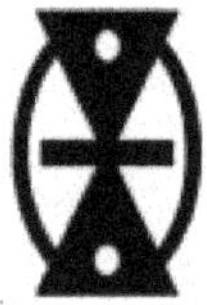 ***Mmere Dane*** Times Change Change or Life's dynamics

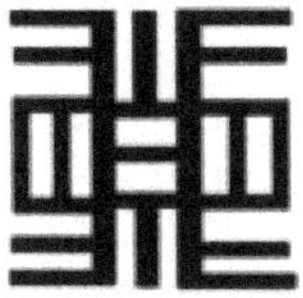 ***Nea Onnim*** He who does not know Knowledge, learning.	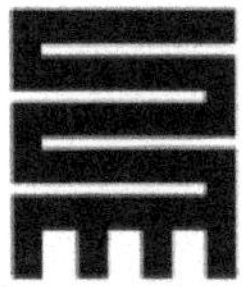 ***Nkyinkyim*** Zigzag Versatility, twist and turns.
 ***Nsoroma*** Star (Child of heaven) Guardianship	 ***Nyame Dua*** Tree of God God's protection
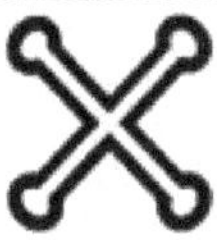 ***Nyame nwu na Mawu*** God will not die for me to die. Immortality of man's soul.	 ***Odo Nyera Fie Kwan*** Love does not miss its way home. Power of love.

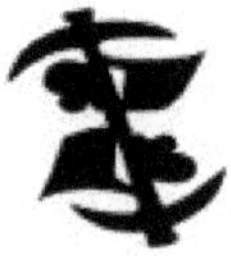 ***Okuafo Pa*** Good Farmer Hard work.	 ***Osram ne Nsoromma*** Moon and star Faithfulness, Love.
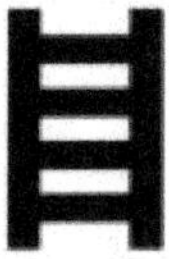 ***Owuo Atwedee*** Ladder of death. Mortality of man.	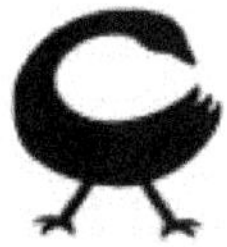 ***Sankofo*** Return for it. Learning from the past.
 ***Tamfo Bebre*** The enemy will suffer. Jealousy and envy.	 ***Sankofa* (Version 2)** Return for it. Learning from the past.

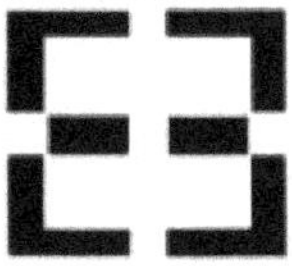 ***Woforo Dua Pa*** When you climb a good tree. Support for good causes.	 ***Sesa Wo Suban*** Change your character. Life transformation.
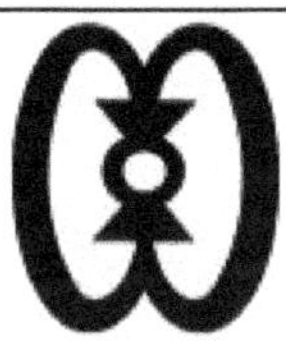 ***Wo Nsa Da Mu*** Your hands are in it. Participatory government.	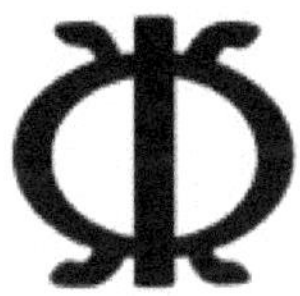 ***Wawa Aba*** Seed of the Wawa Tree. Toughness, perseverance.
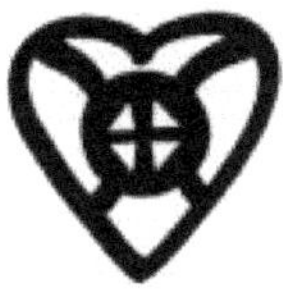 ***Onyankopon Adom*** By God's grace. Hope, providence, faith.	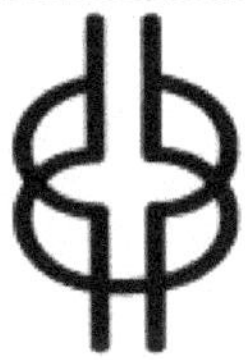 ***Nyansapo*** Wisdom knot Wisdom, intelligence.

 ***Nyame Ye Ohene*** God is King Supremacy of God.	 ***Akofena*** Sword of War Courage and heroism.
 ***Ananse Ntontan*** Spider's web Wisdom and creativity.	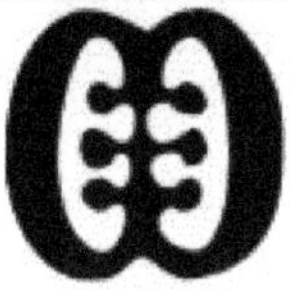 ***Ese Ne Tekrema*** The teeth and the tongue. Inter-dependency
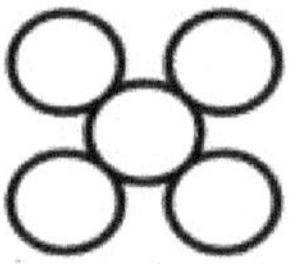 ***Mpuannum*** Five tufts of hair. Symbol of loyalty.	 ***Epa*** Handcuffs. Symbol of law and order.

 ***Mako*** Pepper. Symbol of inequality. .	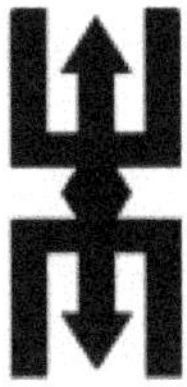 ***Nteasee*** Understanding. Symbol of understanding and cooperation.
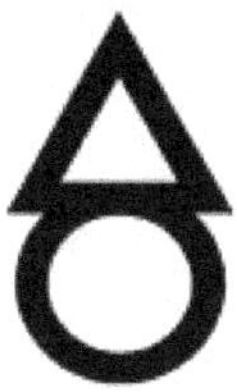 ***Sepow*** Executioner's knife. Symbol of justice.	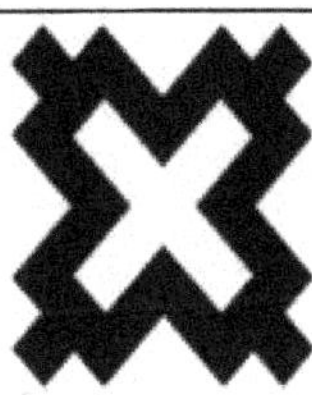 ***Aban*** Fortress. Symbol of authority.

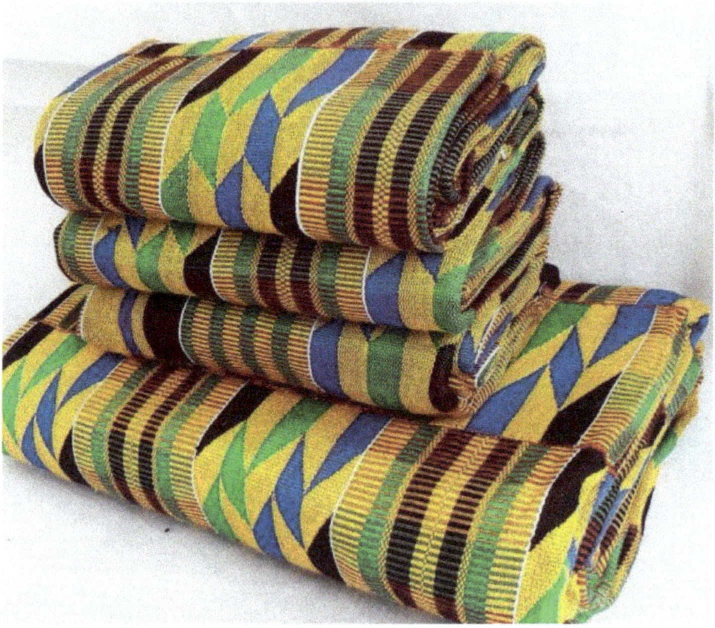

Edwin Asa

Chapter 8

Kente Cloth - Other Uses

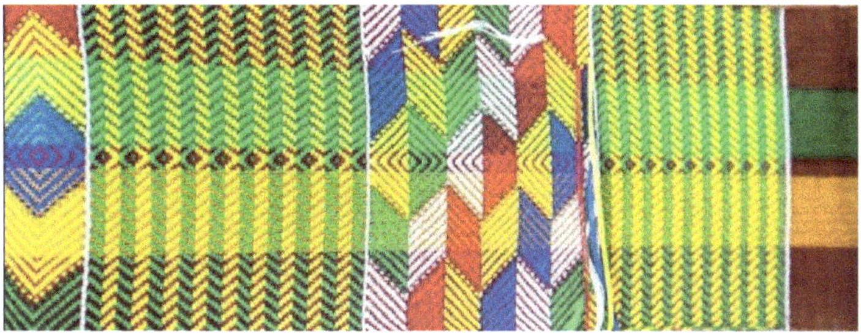

Kente cloth was originally meant to be wrapped around the whole body. This made it extremely uncomfortable for foreigners to use except for decorations. The younger generation also prefer other uses of the Kente cloth like shirts than the actual cloth wrapped around them. Except the villages, people now prefer to wear something that will not be an obstacle to their free movement. Using any of the popular Kente items still portray one's loyalty to the culture and with time the other uses will be far more than the traditional uses except the Chiefs.

Sellers of the cloth started selling just the narrow strips to the numerous tourists that showed interest in the cloth and soon designers started using Kente cloth for a lot of other things. Kente is now found in numerous items. Some of the most popular Kente objects are listed below.

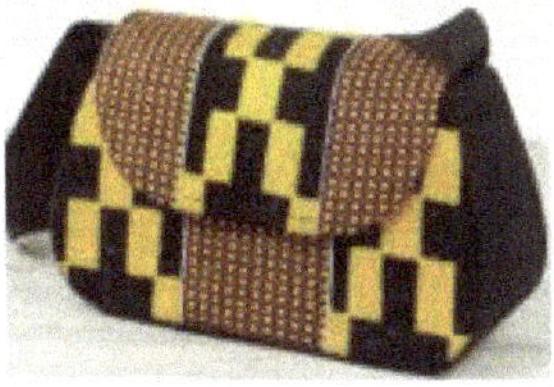 Kente Bag	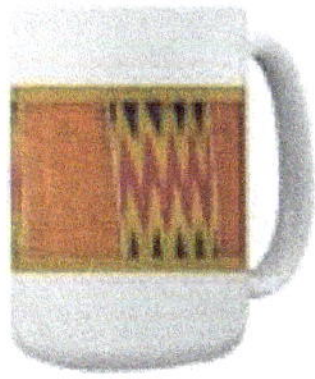 Kente Cup
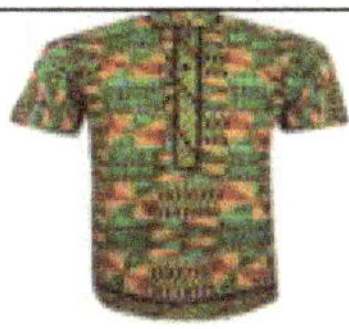 Kente Shirt	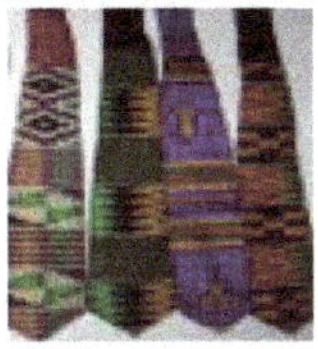 Kente Long Ties
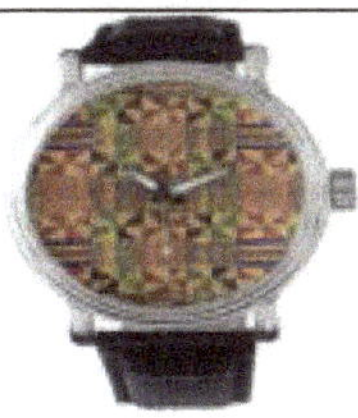 Kente Wristwatch	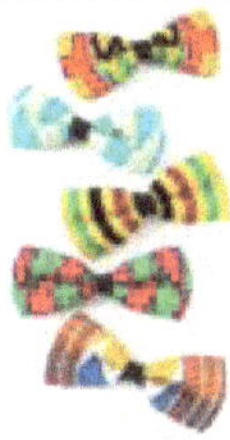 Kente Bow Ties
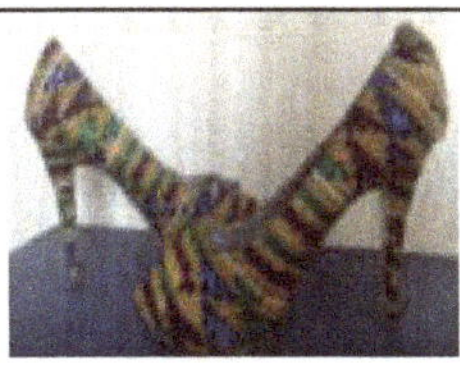 Kente Shoes	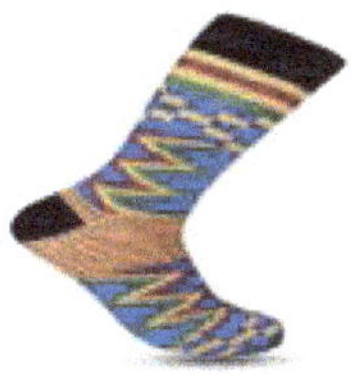 Kente Socks

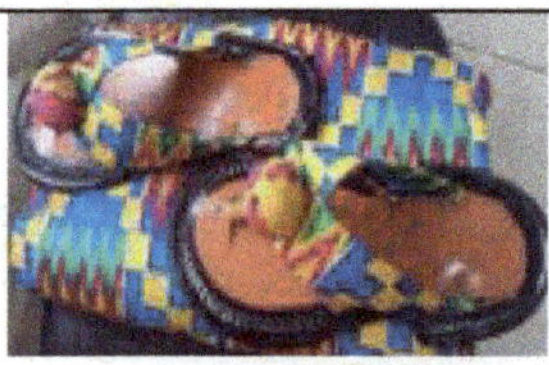 Kente Native Sandals	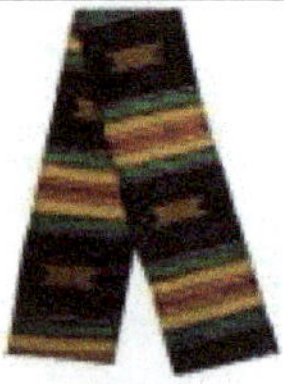 Kente Stole
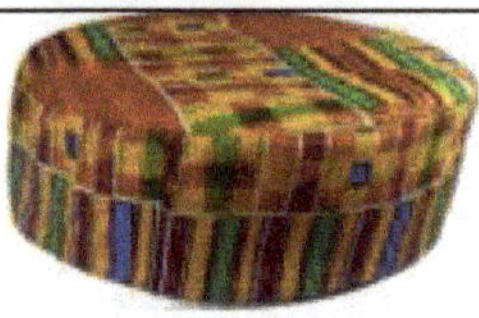 Kente Hat	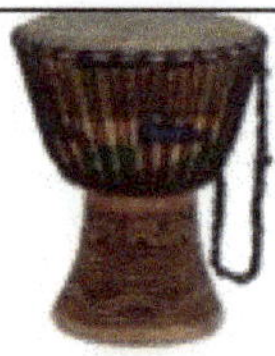 Kente Drum
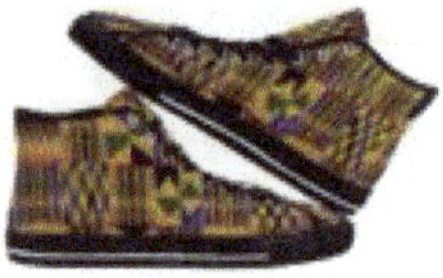 Kente Sneakers	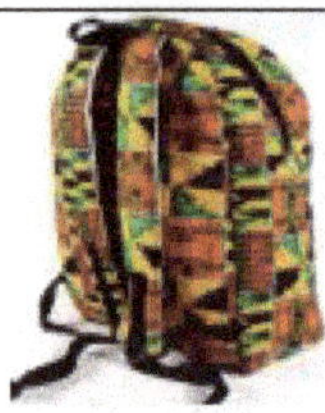 Kente Backpack
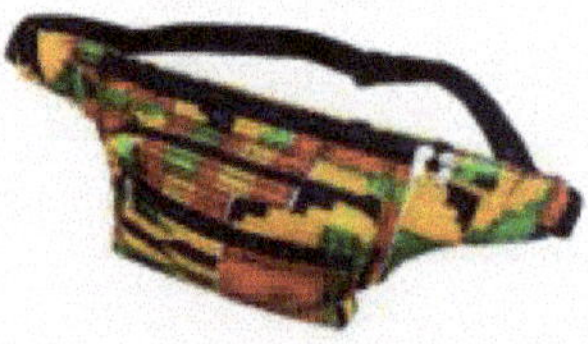 Kente Waist Bag	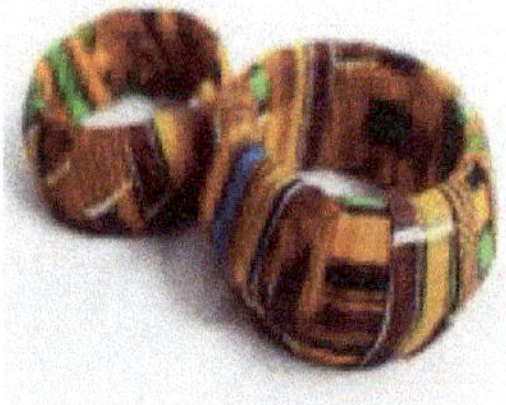 Kente Bracelet

Chapter 9

Kente Cloth and Foreigners

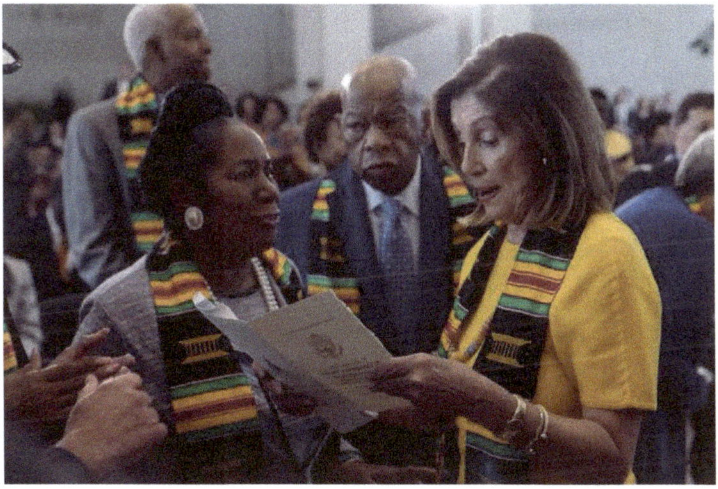

Kente cloth is not the official wear in Ghana. It is also not the official wear for the Asantes. It used to be the royal cloth which later became affordable to others who are not royals. It is however the most presented Ghanaian gift to dignitaries when they visit Ghana. Ghanaian leaders have also presented Kente to their hosts on foreign visits. It is not common for the male

Kente recipients to use them, unlike the female recipients who can easily find use for these gifts.

Some popular foreigners in Kente.

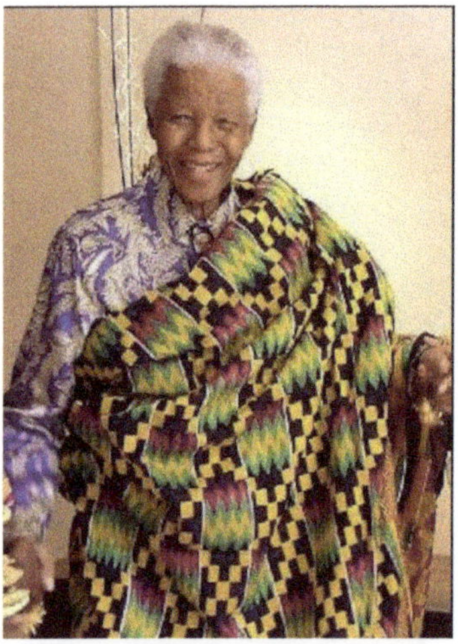

South African President – Nelson Mandela

This Kente cloth was presented to Nelson Mandela by the Asante King Otumfuo Nana Osei Tutu II.

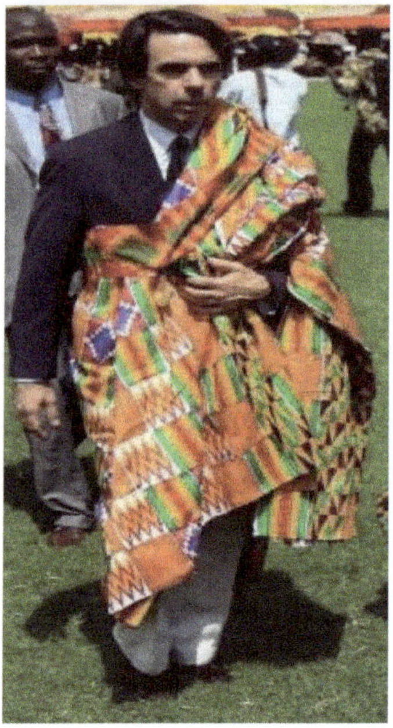

Spanish President – José María Aznar

(1996 – 2004)

The former Spanish president at an Asante Durbar in Ghana.

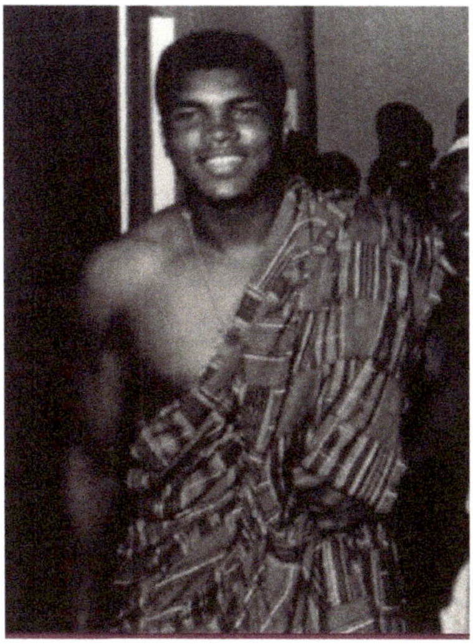

Heavy Weight Boxing Champion – Muhammad Ali.

This Kente cloth was presented to Muhammad Ali by the President of Ghana Dr. Kwame Nkrumah in 1964.

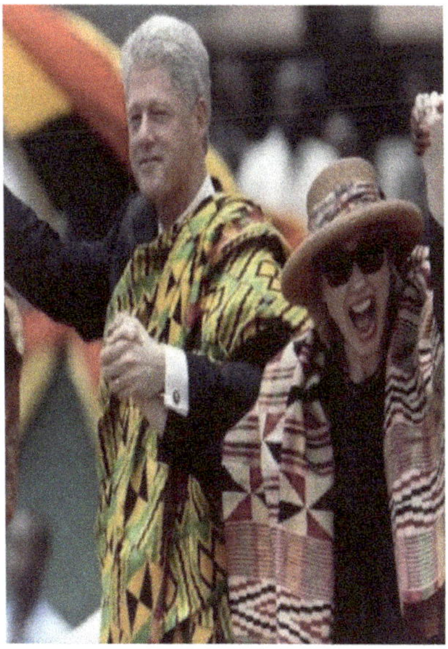

42nd US President – Bill Clinton

This Kente cloth was presented to Bill Clinton by the President of Ghana Flt. Lt. Jerry John Rawlings in March 1998.

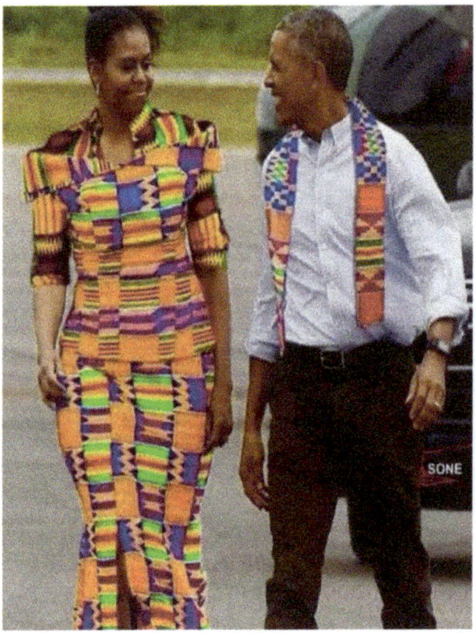

44th US Presisent Barack Obama and wife Michelle Obama

During the first visit to Africa by President and Mrs. Obama in July 2009.

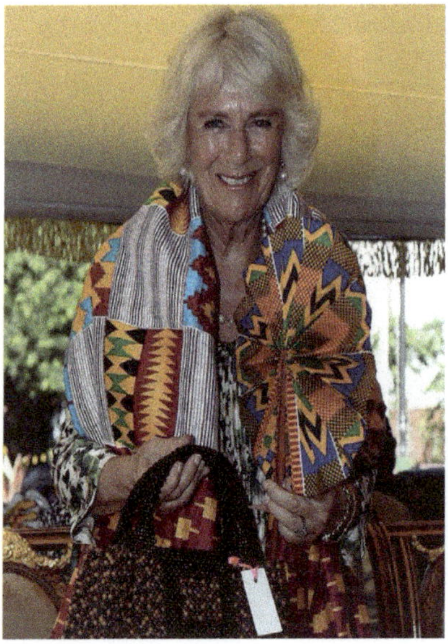

Duchess of Cornwall - Camilla Rosemary Shand

The Duchess was presented with a Kente scarf and bag by the Asante King's wife Lady Julia during a visit to the Manhyia Palace in 2018.

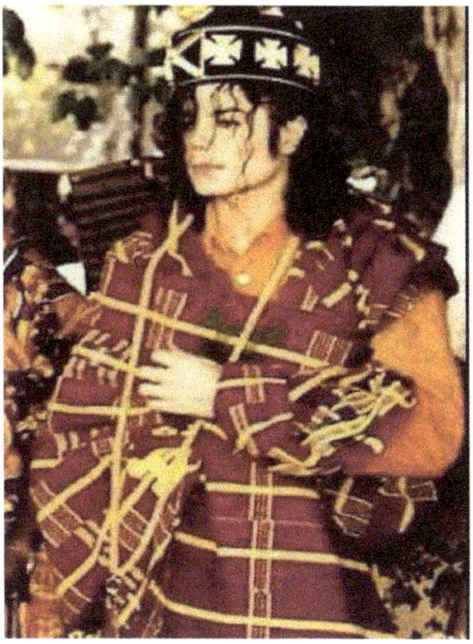

King of Pop Music – Michael Jackson

King of pop crowned honorary King Sani in a ceremony in the village of Krindjabo, Cote d'Ivoire (formally Ivory Coast).

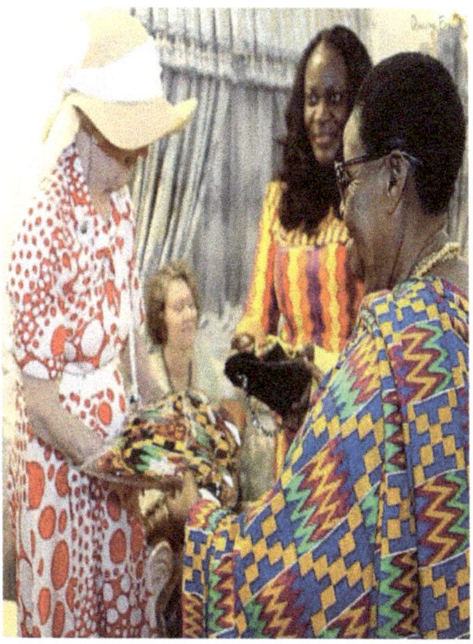

Queen of Denmark Queen Margrethe I

This Kente cloth was presented to the Queen of Denmark by the people of Akwamufie.

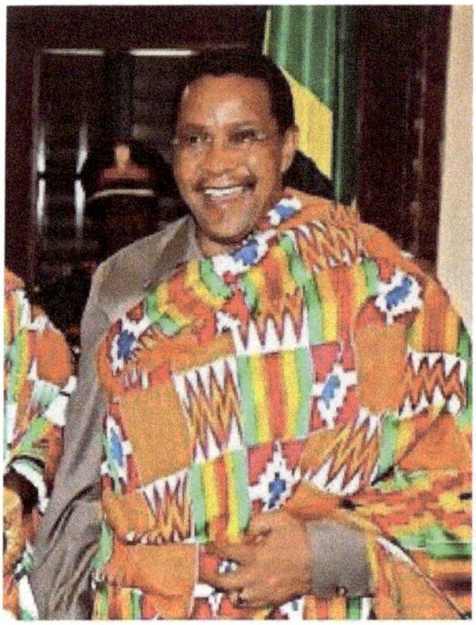

4th President of Tanzania – Jakaya Mrisho Kikwete

This Kente cloth was presented to President Jakaya Kikwete by the Asante King Otumfuo Nana Osei Tutu II.

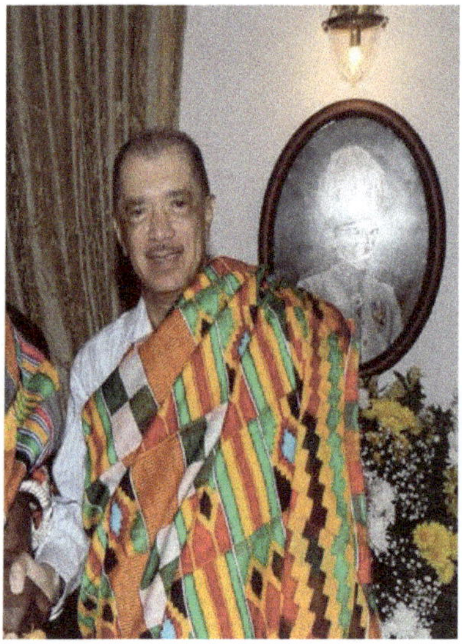

Seychelles President – James Michel

This Kente cloth was presented to President James Michel by the Asante King Otumfuo Nana Osei Tutu II.

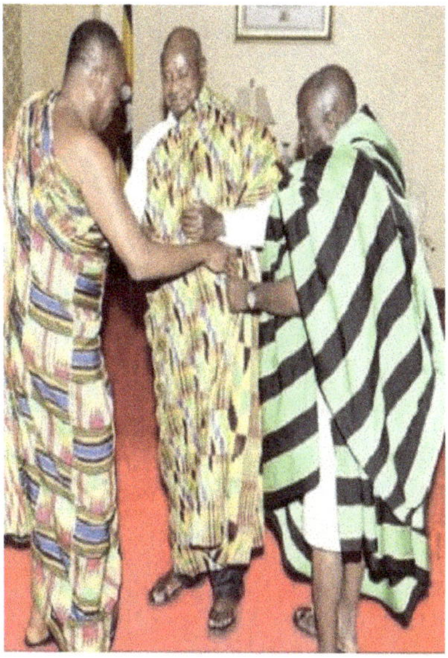

Uganda President - Yoweri Museveni

This Kente cloth was presented to President Museveni by the Asante King Otumfuo Nana Osei Tutu II during the King's visit to Uganda.

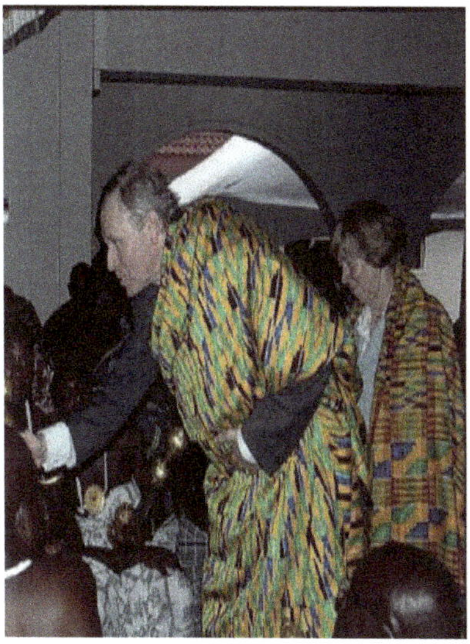

Nato Secretary General (2004-2009) – Dr. Jaap De Hoop Scheffer

Dr. Jaap de Hoop and Mrs. Jeannine de Hoop wrapped in Kente paid a visit to the Manhyia Palace in November 2008.

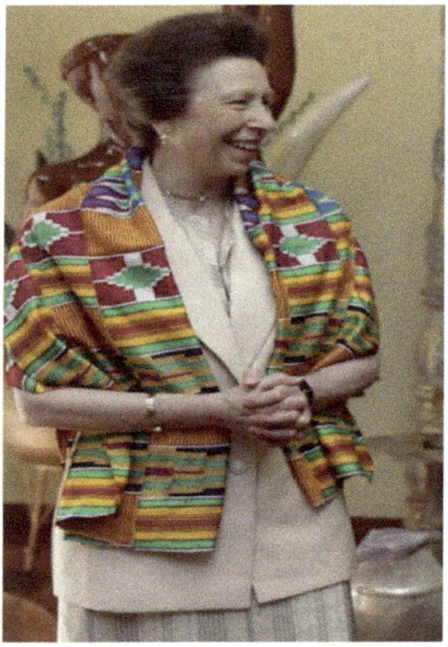

The Princess Royal Anne.

The Princess Royal attending a traditional Durbar ceremony to meet with the Asantehene His Majesty Otumfuo Osei Tutu II in April 2017.

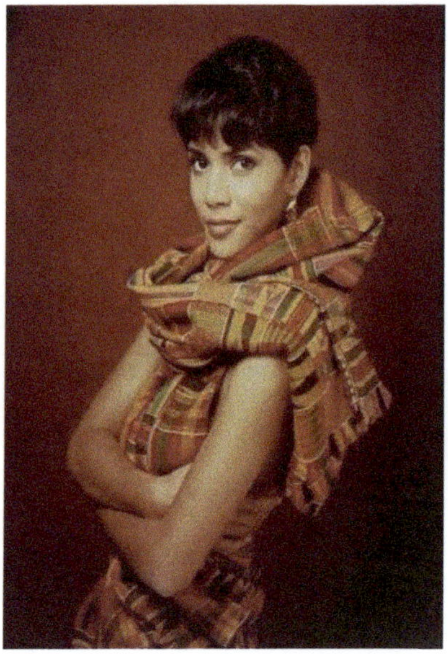

American Actress Halle Berry.

American actress Halle Berry proudly wrapped in the Kente cloth from Bonwire, Ghana.

Chapter 10

Kente Cloth Weaving – Future

The first President of Ghana, Dr. Kwame Nkrumah, and his Cabinet in a show of patriotism through Kente.

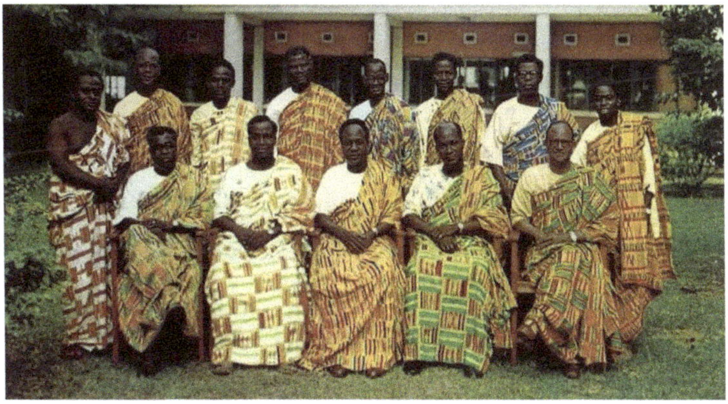

The Prime Minister, Hon Kwame Nkrumah, LLD, MP (centre, seated), and his cabinet. Standing, left to right: Hon A. Ofori Atta, MP; Hon N. A. Welbeck, MP; Hon B.Yeboah Afari, MP; Hon J. H. Allassani, MP; Hon J. B. Erzuah, MP; Hon L. R. Abavana, MP; Hon Ako Adjei, MP; Hon Krobo Edusei, MP. Seated, left to right: Hon A. E. Inkumsah, MP; Hon Kojo Botsio, MP; Hon Kwame Nkrumah, LLD, MP; Hon K. A. Gbedemah, MP; Hon A. Casely Hayford, MP

Kente cloth has been worn in Ghana for over 400 years. In the early years it was only royals who were able to adorn this precious cloth. Today, students display it during their graduations. Kente has gained international status. The most recent exposition was when the US democrats adorned it during a ceremony honoring George Floyd. This single event introduced more people to Kente than the Kente festival in Bonwire itself. The popularity of the Kente cloth is not in dispute. With time it has moved from being popular in Ghana, especially the Akan areas of Ghana to all countries. Kente cloth is meant to be worn by the men with the cloth wrapped around the whole body. This is extremely uncomfortable for non-Ghanaians. Recently Kente has been used in items such as Shirts, Fugu and Scarfs making it easier for more men to use it. The reasons why Kente is so attractive and will stand the test of time are manifold.

Kente is popular because of its beauty. The various pattern of colors and geometric designs make the cloth incredibly unique and beautiful. People are fascinated by the way the threads are intertwined to make all those designs. The combination of the colors used are also quite amazing. The whole weaving process is unique. Watching a master weaver in the weaving process will leave a lasting impression on anyone. The rhythm and the sound cannot be described. It is best to witness it.

Kente cloth is one of the few inventions from Africa that has not been hijacked by foreign producers. Printers have come up with African prints with Kente designs, but it does not come close to the original Kente cloth. The foreign prints are noticeably light weight and will never be worn by the men of Ghana, it will only reveal that you have a ridiculously cheap Kente and most people are very particular about their image. The status of a person in Asante culture is gauged by the quality of the Kente they put on.

Apart from the slave castles in Ghana, nothing can compare to attracting more tourists than the Kente weaving industry. Bonwire is the place to visit if you really want to understand the Kente cloth. This is good for Ghana and the people from Bonwire. Unfortunately, Bonwire does not have abundant fertile lands for them to go into large scale farming. There are no Cocoa farms for the children to inherit so each child starts as early as five years to be introduced to Kente weaving. God gave them this precious culture which has sustained them for over 400 years.

For some years now, students from the Kwame Nkrumah University of Science and Technology (KNUST) have tried to invent a machine that will be able to weave Kente. This is a great idea which will reduce the time it takes to weave the cloth. It is my former school and I wish them success. So far, they have not been successful. They have the machine, but it cannot produce all the different designs. It is best for what we call single weaving or the simple Kente cloth designs.

A machine can be set to create a design but Kente weaving is more than that. It requires the master weaver to think of the different patterns in each block and the colors that will make it stand out. There are some special designs that even master weavers are not able to weave. If Kente is made by machines, tourists will also not travel all the way from far away America to come and witness it. It is the hope that any Kente machine invented will rather find a way to mass produce the threads and other raw materials locally and make them cheaper.

People who are trying to connect to Africa have found a cultural item they can use to portray their affection. With more foreigners using the Kente cloth it is only assumed that the demand for Bonwire Kente is going to be high. It is the hope this book has played a small part in promoting this rich tradition just as my grandfather Papa Kwasi Domfe Gyeabuor did by migrating from Bonwire to that small village called Okyinso to introduce the people in that area to the beautiful tradition of Kente weaving.

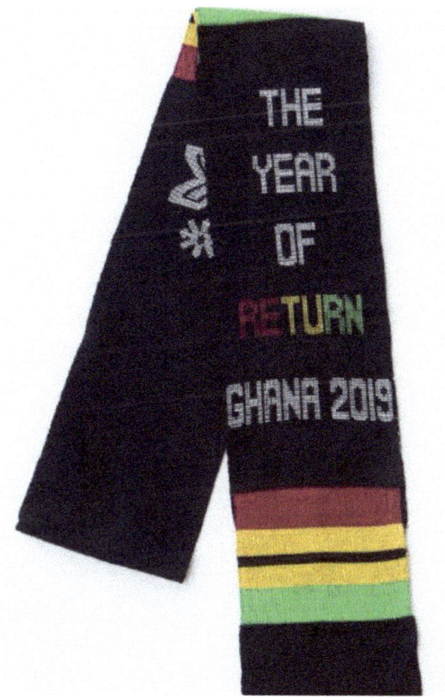

www.ingramcontent.com/pod-product-compliance
Ingram Content Group UK Ltd.
Pitfield, Milton Keynes, MK11 3LW, UK
UKHW062155030826
14089UKWH00025B/22